SCHOOL ESSAYS, LETTERS, PARAGRAPHS, COMPOSITION AND APPLICATIONS

GOODWILL'S

SCHOOL ESSAYS, LETTERS, PARAGRAPHS, COMPOSITION AND APPLICATIONS

Shashi Jain

GOODWILL PUBLISHING HOUSE®
B-3 RATTAN JYOTI, 18 RAJENDRA PLACE
NEW DELHI-110008 (INDIA)

Published by:

GOODWILL PUBLISHING HOUSE®

B-3 Rattan Jyoti, 18 Rajendra Place
New Delhi–110008 (INDIA)
Tel: 25820556, 25750801, 25755559
Fax: 91-11-25764396
Email: goodwillpub@vsnl.net
ylp@bol.net.in
Website: www.goodwillpublishinghouse.com

Printed at:
Kumar Offset
New Delhi

CONTENTS

PART – I

PART – II

PART – III

PART – IV

PART – V

ABOUT THE BOOK

Although many books on school essays and letters are available, but very few explore the creative and free world of children. This book is a joint effort of an authoress and her son, a student. It is a confluence of the conventional art of writing good English and the modern idea of creative freedom. It is a cross-breeding of classical and pop arts of writing essays, letters, applications, paragraphs, composition, notices and advertisements. This presents substance and ideas in a new form, which is interesting and easy flowing. It convinces that every child can express well and write well by looking inwards in his heart and remembering a few basic rules of writing. Writing is not only fun, but also heart-touching. This book is useful for beginners and junior/middle school students.

ABOUT THE AUTHORS

Mrs. Shashi Jain is a freelance author and designer living in New Delhi. She has written numerous articles and books on design, architecture, travel, home science and motherhood.

Ankur Jain is a computer wizard, with an interest in fine arts and writing. He has won several awards in national and international essay and letter writing competitions.

PREFACE

Motivation in writing is not something that comes before the main event like an appetiser. It is a state of initial and continuing awareness by the learner that what he is doing is making him more secure, more able and attractive. To strengthen the child's belief in his ability to make himself understood and appreciated through writing, it is essential to develop his confidence. For this, allow children to develop their ideas through a variety of media. Secondly, physical material available for composition can contribute enormously to children's interest and motivation, as well as to the integrity of their work. The goal of composition writing will be met in an atmosphere in which children can explore their own ideas and express them honestly. But some children will not feel like writing down their thoughts as they are unable to express themselves.

This book is planned for students upto middle school level. It has been designed to help children express themselves. The first part deals with guided compositions, where children are helped with clues, hints, questions or ideas. They are required to understand and expand these ideas and hints.

The second part is paragraph writing in about 150 to 200 words. The ability to write paragraphs should help students in essay writing, which is the next section of the book.

The letter and application writing section is further sub-divided into formal letters, informal letters and applications of very basic nature. The next section deals with notice and advertisement writing where guidelines and situation draft is given. Thus, step-by-step, learning is provided to children.

Authors

INTRODUCTION

The ability to communicate effectively is a major objective of education. It is an asset by which one achieves a frontline position, whether in studies, profession or in any other walk of life. However, with the emerging popularity of telecommunications, particularly mobile phones, television and internet, there is a tendency to ignore the power of writing. The lack of writing skills is a stumbling block in an individual's progress and success.

A commonly believed notion is that writing is a serious literary business. Against this, quite often the essays and letters of novices and children evoke much sincerity and interest. They contain a flavour of freshness and fun. They are often crisp and clear. They have a high probability of spontaneity and express innovative ideas. In fact, too much emphasis on set principles, past trends and model essays robs one of the natural and creative impulse.

We believe that everyone is a born writer. One's creative potential has to be drawn out through proper guidance. This book attempts to provide simple ideas and guidelines for anyone who wants to write through paragraphs, essays, letters, applications, compositions, notices and advertisements

These have been written to cover junior and middle school curriculum.

THE ART OF WRITING

A child learns to talk in an atmosphere of permissive and constructive support. The child strives to express her or his desires and to communicate with others. Everyone tries to help her or him and correct baby talk. After few years of this kind of language the child becomes fluent in speech, adding steadily to his vocabulary, creating original sentences. Even before his schooling, he has developed the underlying structure of spoken language. But written English is taught to the child as a regimented series of business like drills on proper formation of letters. It is found that in three weeks a four-year-old child gets more practice in oral expression than he will get a meaningful writing expression during his entire elementary schooling. The remedy to this situation lies in giving more opportunity to children to practice carefree and spontaneous writing. Composition must be presented as a form of communication and creative expression. All his life he is exchanging ideas with his friends, family and colleagues. He talks and others listen. He may think that he only takes part in a conversation when he is speaking, but he is also taking part when he listens. When he listens, he forms his ideas. Sometimes the idea is unbelievable and at other times the speaker says it as a part of a story. While he is listening, all the time he is developing concepts. He is thinking, posing questions—verbally and mentally. It helps in developing his vocabulary. Therefore, to be a careful listener is one of the first tasks to learn. So, step one is preparation to listen and understand. Step two is to think and set questions. They can be in the form of small questions and related clues, hints or ideas. The questions are so framed that children are able to answer them without difficulty. They must be easy and in simple language.

A composition programme for small children must begin by bringing certain basic questions into focus. The composition programme for young children should be based on communication in the broad sense—on speech in particular and on experience. A child's thinking is usually ahead of his speaking, and speaking is always ahead of his writing. Unfortunately, our writing instructions are skill-bound and rarely for expressing ideas. We should not discourage children from talking or writing simply. In communication, the message comes first. If a child knows that we respect his ideas he will want to express them, and eventually to work to express them more effectively. So, motivation is the key to an effective composition programme. The students should have enough choice and some responsibility. It is wise to allow the students to express their ideas in their own words. They should be encouraged towards the goals that are concerned with quality in both thinking and writing.

The ability to think and write well enables one to respond to any situation and communicate with ease, clarity and flow. For this, the following ground rules should always be remembered:

Observation and perception—Clear and fresh observation should be encouraged in preference to stereotype thinking and blind prejudices.

Honesty in expression—The quality of truthful reporting of what one sees, feels and thinks should be emphasised.

Honesty develops most freely in a friendly and permissive atmosphere, where a child knows that his opinion is worthy of consideration.

Order and design—Every child should be helped to analyse and, if possible, explain the order and meaning in the formlessness of daily impressions and experience.

Style—Writing that is down to earth should be encouraged. Language which is pompous, inflated and inexact should be discouraged. The language and sentence construction should be simple, direct and natural.

Accuracy—The ability to convey the message should be stressed.

Originality—The writing should be original. Encouragement should be given to children who dare to be different, who experiment with language, and who surprise their readers with unusual observation, wit and friendly humour.

Unity—An essay must have unity, developing one theme with a definite purpose. The subject must be clearly defined in the mind and kept in view throughout. Nothing that is irrelevant should be admitted. The subject may be treated in different ways.

Brevity—School essays should not be long. They should be brief, concise and expressive.

Personal touch—The composition should reveal personal feelings and opinions.

A composition must be clear and to the point, treating the subject in an orderly manner. Three features are necessary in a good essay or composition—suitable subject matter, proper arrangement and adequate power of expression.

PART – 1

GUIDED COMPOSITION

COMPOSITION–1

Write a simple composition on a visit to a fire station, with the following clues:

1. Class teacher inviting students to visit the fire station
2. What did you see there?
3. Return from the fire station

VISIT TO A FIRE STATION

Yesterday our class teacher told us that we have been invited to visit a fire station. We all cheered happily. In the morning, I carefully packed my lunch and said goodbye to my parents. I went to the fire station with one

of my friends. Some of my other friends had already arrived. The firemen greeted us warmly. They allowed us to go anywhere in the building. I saw some men sliding down a pole to answer a call. That looked easier than it was. When I tried to slide, I came down with a thud. Everyone at the fire station moved quickly. There were many fire brigades ready to move out at short notice. When we came back from the fire station, we all had lunch. It was a day of great excitement. The visit to the fire station was indeed a learning experience. We got to learn fire safety tips.

COMPOSITION–2

You explored a cave while you drifted apart from your friends and lost your way. Write a composition of about 100 words, with the following clues:

Visit to a mountain; darkness; lost the way; cave for shelter; next morning, road back to camp

EXPLORING A CAVE

Last summer I went backpacking in the mountain with some friends. Darkness was beginning to fall when I lost my way. I was fearful of being left behind in the woods at night. With great difficulty I found a small cave. I was thankful to God for the shelter from rain. I sat huddled by the side of the opening, waiting for help from outside. Finally, I fell asleep. I woke up the next morning and a lovely light crossed my face. The sun has risen and there, just one hundred feet from the cave, was the road back to the camp. Though this experience was adventurous but was scary also. I would always remember this incidence.

COMPOSITION–3

Write a composition in about 150 to 200 words on illiteracy. For your guidance follow the sequence given below:

1. Problem of illiteracy
2. Real facts
3. Causes
   (a) High birth rate
   (b) Official thinking and planning failure
   (c) Education and illiteracy—two different issues
4. Remedial measures
   (a) Spread of literacy
   (b) Network of primary schools
   (c) Social, educational centres and night schools for adults
   (d) Functional literacy centres for adults

ILLITERACY

After independence, one of the challenges before the country was to eradicate illiteracy among the masses. Even after six decades of independence, it still remains a challenge. Although in terms of percentage the ratio of illiterates has dropped, in actual numbers there are more illiterates in India today than six decades ago. It is a fallacy that illiteracy is due to high birth rate and poverty. It is vice versa, that is, high birth rate is due to illiteracy. It is, therefore, not out of place to say that spread of literacy is essential for social and economic development.

Unfortunately, education and literacy are considered synonymous. The government has to plan to give education to all sectors. Its mission to spread education, even to the remotest village, is an uphill task. But the literacy programme is something different. It calls for a different approach and a less leisurely blueprint. One of the remedial measure which is more appropriate for literacy is part-time, easily accessible and flexible educational centres for those who cannot attend or afford regular schools. Besides these, functional literacy centres for adults in semi-urban and rural areas are required where they can learn after their work. For this work non-governmental and voluntary bodies can be very effective and successful than the formal, government setup. People require motivation and personal touch. The tutors have to understand their limitations and priorities to earn a livelihood. As such, the courses have to be interesting and flexible, with adjustable timings.

COMPOSITION–4

Rakesh is a naughty boy. Yesterday he pulled the tail of a stray dog. Mrs. Rao, his mother's friend saw this. Write a paragraph of about 120 words reporting what Mrs. Rao saw and what she told Rakesh.

[A few clues: Stop ... bite you ... doctor will give you injections ... painful ... Besides ... dog is harmless ... unkind ... How would you feel if someone were to pull your hair?]

A NAUGHTY BOY

Rakesh is a naughty boy. Yesterday he pulled the tail of a stray dog. Mrs. Rao, his mother's friend, saw this and shouted. "Stop Rakesh! Do not pull the dog's tail. It will bite you. We will have to take you to the doctor.

He will give you fourteen injections in the stomach. They are very painful, Rakesh. Besides, this dog is harmless. It is unkind and bad to treat animals in this way. How will you feel if someone were to pull your hair? Rakesh, surely you would not like it. Be kind to animals and treat them as you would like to be treated by others."

COMPOSITION–5

Answer the questions given below and write a composition in about 150 to 200 words on environmental pollution.

1. Why is there more carbon dioxide in the atmosphere?
2. What is meant by a hole in the ozone layer?
3. How does rubbish cause pollution?

ENVIRONMENTAL POLLUTION

With the changing lifestyles and industrial development, our environment is getting increasingly polluted. The land, water and air are becoming contaminated and unhygienic for sustaining biological systems, that is growth of flora, fauna, vegetation and people. Due to emission of industries and motorised vehicles, the atmosphere is getting polluted with dangerous chemicals in the form of gases. These gases, mainly carbon dioxide, are produced due to burning of fuels such as petrol, diesel, wood, coal, etc.

We are burning wood and cutting down trees which soak up carbon dioxide by way of producing food. This causes the greenhouse effect, which means a warming of global temperature. Hence, leading to the deadly global

warming. It also causes soil erosion and floods which destroy forests, villages and cities. People and animals in such area face starvation, homelessness and illness. Ozone layer is a protective layer around the earth's atmosphere, which absorbs or reflects the ultraviolet radiation of the sun. It shields us from harmful ultraviolet rays. If they are allowed to filter through too much, they would cause eye and skin diseases and damage crops, flora and fauna. The ozone layer is threatened by using chemicals called CFCs. These chemicals are used in air conditioners, spray cans, fridges and to make plastic items such as fast food boxes. The CFCs are making holes in the ozone layer, which is a serious threat to our environment.

A major environmental pollutant is the fast increasing non-biodegradable waste. With new industrial products and packings, there is a sudden spurt in throwaway materials such as plastics, cans, bottles, packings, bags, etc. Many of these items are non-biodegradable and dangerous. They pollute water and land and accumulate on the earth as eyesores. They not only create pollution but also occupy valuable land space, which otherwise can be used for greenery or human habitat for the benefit of people.

COMPOSITION–6

On family planning day, the prime minister gave a message to the nation. Write a composition with the following points:

1. Every child has the right to proper care and education
2. Most children do not get parental care
3. No parent wants to neglect his children but is helpless because of large numbers
4. The children, parents and nation suffer
5. Need of family planning
6. How non-government organisations, voluntary agencies and government can play an important role

MESSAGE ON FAMILY PLANNING

Every child, whether he belongs to the rich or poor, has a right to proper care from his parents. He or she has the right to have food, clothing, education and other basic necessities of life. It is sad that millions of children grow up without parental care. They grow up on their own.

It is not that the parents want to neglect their offsprings, but they are helpless. Many parents find it difficult to provide the bare necessities of life because of large families. They work from morning to evening and do not have time to look after their children. The ultimate sufferers are the children, the parents and the nation. No nation can progress where children do not have access to basic needs of life, education and a stable background.

As such, for our country, family planning acquires a most urgent priority. It is the need of the hour. We have to educate and persuade each family, even in the remotest area, to adopt family planning and restrict their family size. We have to tell them the measures of birth control. In this task non-government organisations and voluntary agencies can play an important role. It is for us in the government to launch a movement to convince people about the importance of family planning.

Today, let us take a pledge that we will help in carrying the message of family planning to the remotest villages. Please accept my best wishes and I appeal to all sections of society to adopt family planning for the sake of their children, their families and the nation.

COMPOSITION–7

Use the points given below and write a composition in about 150 words.

1. A large bird with a yellowish patch beneath the neck
2. Existing population is too small and decreasing fast
3. Stork has survived only in Assam and is usually found in plains flooded by the Brahmaputra
4. An endangered species because:

(a) Its eggs are stolen
(b) Villagers cut the trees on which storks make their nests
(c) The village garbage dumps from which storks usually eat are most unhygienic

STORK—AN ENDANGERED SPECIES

Stork is a beautiful large bird with a long neck. It has 19 living species and most of them are migratory. It is an endangered species, which means that like tiger, lion, cheetah and zebra, it is also on the verge of extinction. The present population of storks is quite alarming; the numbers are too small and also decreasing rapidly. Previously they were present in Bharatpur Bird Sanctuary in large numbers. But due to indiscriminate killings and changing environment, they are fast disappearing. At present they are only found in the plains of Assam, which are flooded by the River Brahmaputra.

Storks are an endangered species because of several reasons. Firstly, their eggs are stolen by the villagers, tourists and hunters. Secondly, due to cutting of trees for fuel and other purposes, the nests of the storks are being destroyed. Lastly, the food the storks eat is usually unhygienic. Storks eat the food from the village dumps, which are most unhygienic and full of plastics, trash and rotten stuff. In the process, the population of the storks is dwindling drastically.

There is a need to make emergency efforts to save storks from extinction. For this purpose, the law against their hunting is not adequate. They are part of the natural ecosystem. As such, the primary need is to maintain the natural balance of the flood plains and swamps of the Brahmaputra Valley and not to allow any tree cutting.

COMPOSITION–8

Write a report on your English course book. Suggested outline:

1. Title
2. Author
3. Publisher
4. Year published
5. Number of pages
6. The unit/stories/poems you like the most
7. The reason you like them
8. Do you enjoy doing the exercises in this book?

YOUR ENGLISH COURSE BOOK

Communicative English is a comprehensive and innovative course, comprising of a course book, a workbook and a literary reader. They constitute integral items of the language package. It is written by Professor P.K. Ram and Paul D'souza, who are associated with the Prime Institute of English and Foreign Languages, Chennai. It was first published in the year 2005 by Knowledge Publishers and printed by ABC Printers, New Delhi. Since then it is published every year with a revised edition. The course book contains 119 pages, the workbook 50 pages and the literary reader 149 pages. It has nine units. Each unit is based on one central theme. The units are presented through different genres, like stories, plays, poems and informative pieces and are full of tasks and activities. These help to develop four basic communicative language skills, which are listening, speaking, reading and writing, alongwith the ability of thinking.

The book has step-by-step learning and a thematic approach. The introduction serves as an appetiser.

The book is full of good stories such as The Adventures of Toto, Moti Guj, The Lost Child, David Copperfield, The Stir Outside the Cafe Royal, The Adventures of Tom Sawyer, On a Saturday Morning, etc. I like the Adventures of Tom Sawyer the most. It is a story of a naughty boy, Tom, who lives with his aunt Polly. His aunt loves him a lot but sometimes punishes him. The story revolves around naughty Tom, who steals jam and escapes beatings due to his presence of mind. She punishes him by making him work on Saturday, which is a holiday. I like the way the writer, Mark Twain, presents the boy, Tom, who with his intelligence and presence of mind not only makes others work, but in the process acquires small articles, such as an apple, twelve marbles, a tin soldier, a key, a dog's collar, the handle of a knife and four pieces of an orange. He does not work himself but the fence still has three coats of paint.

I also enjoy doing the worksheets. They are interesting and easy to do. By doing them the student improves his grammar. It helps in a better vocabulary and pronunciation. The worksheet also helps me to communicate better.

COMPOSITION–9

Imagine you are Ajita. Write a short composition describing how you won an award, what you felt when you received the award and what are your plans for the future.

A BRAVE DEED

I am Ajita. I am ten years old and live in a village of Bastar, Madhya Pradesh. On Saturday afternoon my younger brother Ajay was playing. I was reading a story book. My mother was preparing tea for my aunt, who had come to visit us. My younger brother, who is four years old, is very fond of music. He wanted to play a tape recorder that had a damaged lead. As soon as he switched on the tape recorder, he suffered a severe electric shock and got stuck to the electric switch board. He shouted and my mother and aunt ran towards him. They were trying to pull him away, but were also stuck to the switch board. I remembered that wood is a bad conductor of electricity. So, I used a wooden stick to pull the damaged lead out of the socket and thus, I saved three lives.

Next day my uncle reported this incident in a newspaper. Within a few days, I received a letter from the Indian Council of Child Welfare announcing a bravery award. I was very happy and thrilled. My friends and relatives congratulated me. Now I am in Delhi to receive the award. I have come here for the first time and I like the city. I am excited and want to see our national capital. I want to be a police officer so that I can bring peace and security to the nation.

PART – II

PARAGRAPH WRITING

1. MY FIRST DAY IN MIDDLE SCHOOL

Monday, the 15th of April was my first day in class VI of middle school. I was thrilled like a mountaineer, who has to climb and conquer the Himalayas. I was looking forward to a year, where every day is full of adventure and a new chapter of knowledge. It was a day of mixed feelings. I was happy to see most of my friends but also missed those who were given other sections. I could see some new faces with whom I became friendly. On every face I could see a feeling of confidence. The boys and girls were feeling more independent as they had come to the middle school. I felt grown up and responsible. Perhaps the best part of the day was to find a very fine and friendly teacher. A teacher who makes every day a beautiful day. She introduced herself and asked the names of all the students. Her name is Rosy D'souza and she had done her M.A. (English) from a reputed college. She was constantly smiling and cheerful. She made our day. At the same time, I found that most of my classmates felt sad about missing their class teacher of the previous year.

2. THE SCHOOL ASSEMBLY

Most schools follow certain traditions. The school assembly is one such convention. Assembly implies getting together. Students generally assemble in the forecourt of their schools every morning or in some

schools on certain days of every week. They have to wear proper uniforms. Like a military regiment, they have to form queues and stand straight. The ritual invariably includes singing the national anthem, address to the students, presentation of awards and some announcements, sermons and warnings. It is often argued that the assembly is a wonderful occasion to know each other and exchange information. Frankly, I hardly find it a place for communication and interaction. On the contrary, it makes one feel small among thousands in the assembly line of a factory. I am puzzled about the purpose of having regular assemblies. In fact, most of the students find it boring, except on some special occasions, like handing over or taking over of appointments. Since, they wear out young students in the morning, school authorities should consider whether assemblies serve any useful purpose. Maybe some alternative and innovative method of assembly could be evolved which is less cumbersome, more relevant and interesting.

3. MY MOTHER

There are many persons whom I like, but there are few whom I love. Among those whom I love I admire my mother the most. She is the most wonderful person in the world. She is a teacher. She cooks delicious food. I don't admire her just because she is my mother. I admire her just because she is a strong willed and wonderful person. She also likes to write. Her book was presented to the former president of India, Dr. Abdul Kalam. I attended this function and felt very proud of my mother. The president complemented me for having such a talented person as my mother. She loves me and I obey her. She teaches me and helps me with my homework and studies. She consoles me whenever I am depressed. She encourages me whenever I have any difficulty. She gives all her attention to me and our home. When I am not well, she feels terrible. She tries to comfort me, forgoing her rest, sleep and food. She often gets up during the night to see that I am comfortable. She brings attractive clothes for me. She often buys me ice-cream and gifts. At the same time, she tells me not to make it a habit to take too much of fast food. Sometimes, she gets angry when I do not listen to her. But very soon she sheds her anger and forgives me. I can see how difficult it is to be a mother. That is why I love my mother very much and try to be careful not to trouble or annoy her.

4. DIWALI—MY FAVOURITE FESTIVAL

India is a land of festivals. It has a wide variety of cultural, religious and social festivals celebrated throughout the year. People wear new clothes, sing and dance and

enjoy sweets and feasts. Diwali is my favourite festival. It is a festival of lights and joy. Houses, shops and all other buildings are decorated with earthen lamps at night. Almost everyone in India celebrates this festival. People whitewash and paint their homes before diwali. They wear new clothes and buy new utensils. Children are thrilled with lights, crackers and sweets. The homes arc lighted and decorated and people exchange sweets and gifts. People go to temples and worship Laxmi, the Goddess of wealth. On this day Lord Rama returned after killing the demon King Ravana and was coronated as the king of Ayodhya. Also on this day, Lord Krishna killed Nakrasura. On this day, the Jain Lord Mahavira achieved *Nirvana*. Diwali is celebrated at the dawn of winter. The hot summer starts waning. The weather becomes pleasant. After the harvest, farmers start preparing to sow the new crop. Diwali is indeed a beautiful festival, which brings light and joy to all homes and heart.

5. DUSSEHRA

India is a land of distinct cultures and colourful festivals. Each festival in India has its own meaning and purpose of celebration. The festival of dussehra has a religious meaning and inherent values. It is celebrated on *Dashmi* (10th day) of the lunar month of *Ashwin*.

According to the great Indian epic, *Ramayana*, Ravana was a great scholar but a demon. He was the king of Sri Lanka. He was killed on this day by Lord Rama. Bengalis believe that the Goddess Durga came to earth on this day. The meaning of Durga is victory of good over evil. We celebrate dussehra so that our evils are destroyed and goodness triumphs. It connotes ten evils, which man should conquer, as 'duss' means ten and 'hara' means defeat. Dussehra is celebrated in all parts of India with joy and fervour. The effigies of Ravana, his brother Kumbhkarna and his son Meghnatha are burnt. The *Ramayana* is staged and fairs are arranged all over the country. People feast and distribute sweets. Children wear new clothes and get toys and sweets. Dussehra not only brings joy but also inspires us to win over our bad instincts by good deeds and pious thoughts.

6. HOW I CELEBRATE CHRISTMAS

Every year 25th December is celebrated as christmas, the birthday of Jesus Christ world over. It is a festival of feasting, rejoicing and giving and receiving gifts. The festivity begins on christmas eve. I celebrated christmas in my own way. In the morning when I woke up, I looked for socks under my pillow. It had small gifts, toffees, an eraser and pencils. My mother told me that these are gifts from Santa Claus, but actually I know my parents keep these gifts for me. I made greeting cards and a painting of Santa Claus. My mother made cakes and pudding. We bought a christmas tree and decorated it with bulbs, bells and balloons. I invited my friends home in the evening and we sang christmas carols and enjoyed cakes and other goodies. We did not forget the poor. We served food to

the poor children of our locality. We also distributed old woollen clothes to the street children. I collected these clothes from my home and neighbours. This is the way I celebrated christmas last year. I am keenly looking forward to christmas this year also.

7. A CROWDED MARKET STREET

It was around diwali. We wanted to buy clothes, decorative lights and many other items. Chandni Chowk is famous for such things. My mother asked me to join her and see for myself what this famous market is like. Chandni Chowk is near the Red Fort in Old Delhi. There was a huge crowd there. Everyone was pushing each other. There were traffic jams and vehicles were blowing their horns. Street vendors were selling various items which were very cheap. They were shouting on top of their voices to attract customers for their wares. Many customers were bargaining with the shopkeepers. We

went to a saree shop where my mother bought a saree. She bought some artificial jewellery. We also bought some sweets from a famous sweet shop. From the electrical market we bought lights and a mixer-juicer. I also bought some records, CDs of classical music and some toys. We were tried after shopping. We had cold drinks and some snacks to refresh ourselves. Thereafter we returned home. I enjoyed the shopping very much, although the market was very crowded.

8. THE CRAFTS MUSEUM

India is a unique country which has a rich variety of crafts. It has a long tradition and widc rangc of handicrafts. These include textiles, pottery, toys, jewellery, woodwork, sculpture, paintings, metal-work, leather-work, etc. The Crafts Museum in Delhi provides a panorama of the traditional crafts from various parts of the country. The Crafts Museum is situated in Pragati Maidan. It exhibits the styles of houses of various regions of India. It has a gallery which displays the beautiful crafts of old cultures. There are artists and craftsmen, working at the museum, who make beautiful items. One can see the weaving of colourful sarees and carpets, making of pottery and toys etc. It is amazing to see magical hands carving a stone or a wooden sculpture. Rural artisans from Bihar make attractive Madhubani paintings. The artisans from Orissa, West Bengal, Rajasthan, Gujarat, Andhra Pradesh, Tamil Nadu and other states demonstrate their talents and skills in handicrafts and various other arts. One can have a glimpse of a miniature India at the Crafts Museum. I felt very proud of my country after I visited this museum.

9. MY SUMMER HOLIDAY IN SHIMLA

It was summer. Delhi was scorching hot, while the mountains were cool. We decided to go to Shimla. Mummy did the packing and daddy got the train tickets. We went by train to Kalka. From there, we took the famous mini train. It reaches Shimla in five hours, passing over mountains. There are 107 tunnels on the way. The journey by this train was very exciting. It was already quite cool. At 5 pm we reached Shimla. We rested in the hotel for a couple of hours. After dinner we went for a walk on the Mall Road. There were many people on this road. Being on the hill, one has to go up and down. There was a lift on the Mall Road. A tired person can use the lift rather than climbing up and down. Chadwick Waterfalls near Summer Hill was a pleasant picnic spot. We reached there by trekking next day. We took a bath in the icy water at the falls. Jhaku is the highest hill of Shimla. It has a temple. There were a lot of monkeys all

around the temple. They like grams and bananas, which I gave them to eat. They became my friends. We went to see the museum. It had old statues, paintings, coins, jewellery, guns and many interesting things. After four days of fun and frolic we returned home.

10. HOW I NEED TO SPEND MY HOLIDAYS

During the holidays one is free to do what one likes. One has all the time for entertainment or to learn something new. There is complete choice and freedom. But this does not mean that we should waste our time. We should make the best use of time by developing new skills, learning many things besides playing and enjoying holidays. During holidays, I wish to spend at least one hour every day in writing articles for newspapers and magazines. To improve my health, I would like to spend two hours daily on sports and physical exercise. I am planning to go to Panchmarhi for a week. There, I will go trekking and make an ecological study. Nowadays, computers have become very popular and indispensable. I will try to learn some basics about computers. One has lots of time for various entertainments, playing and pursuing his hobbies. I would like to swim to beat the heat and keep cool. I am also thinking of practising the guitar, doing some gardening and enlarging my coin and stamp collection. I also intend to study several encyclopedias to improve my general knowledge. Holidays provide an opportunity to learn many new things. Beside this, holidays can be an experiment to learn how to plan our time and become self-reliant.

11. MY PET ANIMAL

A pet is a domesticated animal or bird. People keep pets for their pleasure. Pets are good company for lonely people. There are many kinds of pets—like dog, cat, rabbit, and bird. I have a pet dog. She is as white as snow, so we call her Snowy. She is very beautiful and smart. She possesses a small body with agile eyes. She is like a member of our family. She loves all of us and shares our moments of joy and sorrow. She responds well to my call. She waits for me to return from school. She enjoys playing with the ball, but dislikes taking a bath. During occasional tragedies and moments of grief, she becomes very sad and refuses to eat. Sometimes she acts mischievously and teases us. Snowy has certain natural instincts. She performs various jobs like picking up the newspaper, calling daddy for dinner and guiding my grandfather to the market. She has an extremely sensitive nose for food, animals and people. She can recognise strangers and unwelcome visitors. She has a keen sense of hearing. She wags her tail when she is happy or when I return from school. Though small in body, Snowy is strong, agile and intelligent. Snowy has clean habits. She does not make the house dirty. She eats in her plate. I feed her bread and chapatis. She is very fond of mangoes and sweets. She often goes with me for an evening walk and we play together, hop, run and jump. She makes friends with children. She is not only a member of our family, but like a doll. She has taught us to love animals as they also have sentiments and feelings like human beings.

12. THE RAINY DAY

The earth was hot and the sun was burning. The trees were wilting and the birds appeared to be lifeless. Everyone was eagerly looking forward to the monsoon. It was a surprise when suddenly the sky became overcast.

Soon, with a clap of thunder the rain started. The earthy smell of the raindrops hitting the hot earth started wafting around. Lifeless trees came back to life. The rain washed the buildings and roads. People, cars, buildings and trees looked attractive with their reflections in the pools of clear water. People with bright umbrellas and raincoats of various colours presented a beautiful scene. Birds started singing and peacocks were dancing. Children were playing, singing and dancing with joy. Everyone was happy to see the rain. When the rain stopped, a beautiful rainbow appeared in the sky. The rainy day was like a dream come true and a great relief from the scorching heat.

13. 'SAVE FOR A RAINY DAY'

For our holiday homework, my English teacher asked us to write a paragraph on 'Save For a Rainy Day'. I did not know what this meant. I felt like having been caught in the rain. One morning, I asked my mother what it meant. We were sitting in the balcony. She pointed towards the squirrel, whom we feed peanuts and grams every day. It lives with its brood in the trunk of a nearby tree. It had stored a lot of nuts and other food in its house. My mother said that it was just preparing for the time when it may not get anything to eat due to rain. In other words, so that it may not be 'caught in the rain'. The squirrel and its family would not be without food, even if it rains. When it is not possible to go out to fetch food, they can use the nuts stored in their house. Being prepared is what 'Saving For a Rainy Day' means. One should always save something to bank upon during bad times. Wise people always plan ahead and are prepared for any eventuality. Everyone can learn from the squirrel and always be prepared with savings. If they do not, they will be 'caught in the rain'.

14. PICNIC IN THE RAIN

It was a fine sunny day. The air was cool and the weather was pleasant. We thought that we would be wasting such a nice day indoors. I contacted my friends and we all started on our bikes for a picnic. Full of excitement, we were singing and enjoying. While we were halfway, suddenly it became dark and clouds covered the sky. Before we could think of doing anything, the clouds started thundering fiercely. It was like the roar of a pride of lions. It was literally a cloudburst, with a big bang. Our hearts filled with fear and all plans of picnic sank like a paperboat in the river. All our excitement vanished. We were completely soaked in the rain and so was our food. Everyone was sad, perplexed and quiet. Then I thought that instead of cursing nature, we could enjoy this unexpected event. My friends agreed and we started bathing, playing, and dancing in the rain. We sang classical ragas of monsoon. While people were running helter-skelter, we were enjoying the rains. It was an enchanting scene, looking at the colourful umbrellas, people soaked in the rain, ground covered by water and everything, including trees, taking the shower. The reflection of colours, patterns and light in the water, under the vast umbrella of the overcast sky, was making a wonderful scene. It was like a picture by modern painter. This is the most memorable but unexpected picnic of my life.

15. THE HAPPIEST DAY OF MY LIFE

When I think of my life, there have been many happy days like my birthday, getting prizes, festivals and celebrations. But the happiest day of my life is the day I gave a music performance for the first time on stage. The date was 3rd March, 2010. Mother's International School had organised an inter-school classical music competition. Many students from different schools in Delhi participated in this event. Some students rendered vocal songs, while some budding artists played the tabla, harmonium and tanpura. The little artists enthralled the audience with the guitar, veena and sitar. Then, it was my turn. It was my first performance on stage. I felt very nervous and prayed to God. However, once I started singing I forgot everything. I was totally engrossed in rendering *Raag Behaag*. I even forgot that the audience was listening to me till there was loud clapping in the auditorium. I was thrilled with joy when my name was announced for the first prize. I was given a gold medal by the chief guest. I felt very proud and happy. This was the happiest day of my life.

16. AN ACCIDENT

It was a pleasant sunny day during winter. We had gone to Chennai and I was keen to see the sea. So we went to the beach. We hired a boat and went sailing. Many other people were also enjoying boating and fishing. There were some motorboats also. Suddenly a motorboat came very close to our boat at a very high speed. It created strong waves. This turned one of the boats with fishermen, upside down. The boat started sinking in the sea.

However, out of six fishermen four were saved by another boat, but two fishermen were not found. Perhaps, they drowned in the sea. I was frightened to see this accident. I felt afraid of the water and we returned to the shore. Since that day I am frightened of the sea and motorboats. The picture of this accident flashes before my eyes, whenever I see the sea or boats. But I have decided to overcome my fear of sea and boats and be careful while boating. I have also decided to learn swimming to help myself to safety if any accident happens.

17. A GOOD DEED

When I started writing an essay on 'A Good Deed' as a part of vacation homework, my pen stopped. I began to think what good deed of mine I should describe. Should it be feeding the birds or giving alms to beggars occasionally? Can it be serving my parents when they are ill or helping my sister with her work? No, I thought these are insignificant for an essay. I started introspecting my thirteen years of life more deeply. I felt that most of the things I do are for my own self. Playing, studying, reading, watching TV, computers, music, participating in competitions etc., are all for my own benefit. Am I becoming too self-centered? I must confess that I decided to do one good deed so that I could write my essay. It is said, "Where there is a will, there is a way." The same evening I found a small girl crossing the road carelessly. Suddenly, a state transport bus came rushing at high speed, unconcerned with the safety of anyone else. Risking my life, I just ran on the street and pulled the little girl out of the way. Her life was saved. The bus driver stopped the bus and started abusing us. A crowd gathered on the spot and the parents of the girl called the police. On our complaint, the license of the bus driver was cancelled. Although the parents of the girl felt very obliged towards me, I was very happy because I had a reason to write my essay on a good deed.

18. A FRIGHTENING DREAM

It was a windfall. I was thrilled to bag the first prize in a lucky draw. It was a free holiday and travel to the Disneyland. I boarded a Jumbo Jet. Immediately it soared high in the sky. But my joy was shortlived. It kept on going higher and higher. I was terribly frightened. While flying, it crashed into a satellite and broke into pieces. I started falling down. Suddenly, I saw a huge bird as big as a helicopter. I managed to catch its wings. After some time, the bird landed on a ship. I got down on the deck. I was thinking that my life has been saved. But it was not so. Suddenly, there was a big blast and the ship broke into pieces. I tried to save my life by holding on to a wooden plank and swimming. It was on an unending sea, which was full of sharks and whales. I was so frightened that I shouted, "Mummy! Mummy!" As soon as my mother heard my call, she woke me up and asked me what had happened. I was so happy to find that it was only a 'frightening dream'.

19. OUR NOISY NEIGHBOURS

We live in Hauz Khas. There are three other families who live in our building. They are our neighbours. Since early morning our neighbours create a lot of noise. Small babies start crying with full throat. They often wake me up. As soon as they stop, music practice starts with the loud noise of drums and the tabla. The boys in our neighbourhood are very fond of riding on motorbikes, which have no silencers. They also enjoy late night parties with loud music and dance. The ladies are very religious. Every Tuesday they sing religious *bhajans* over the loudspeakers. The noise disturbs me in my study, work and sleep. I sometimes tell them not to disturb us or other neighbours and maintain peace in the locality, but they hardly care. Last week, I was amazed to find complete peace. I was very curious to know what had happened. It was because their daughter fell ill. The doctor advised them not to make any noise or disturb her sleep. Her grandfather had also come to see her and stayed back. Everyone was careful not to disturb the two of them. So, all loud music, loudspeakers and parties stopped. I got an opportunity to tell him about the noise round the clock. He helped me by telling everyone to be more civilised and a bit more considerate towards the neighbours. Since then it has been peaceful and we are all friends.

20. IF I WIN A LOTTERY

The other day I read in the newspaper that an Indian boy in America had won three crores dollars in a lottery. I thought how wonderful and what a lucky chap. If I had won the lottery, I would have been perhaps the richest girl in India. First, I would have given a treat to my entire school. Then, I would have donated Rs. ten lakh to my school. For myself, I would buy a lot of books, clothes and shoes. Also I would buy a luxury car and a farmhouse. In order to earn more money, I would run a large departmental store, something like Kids Kem of Bangalore. I would also use this money for the poor and orphans.

You might be thinking how I can do all this in Rs. three crore. Yes, if I win a lottery, it should be at least Rs. 60 crore.

21. MY ROLE MODEL

India is a great country. She has given birth to great persons like Buddha, Mahavira, Ashoka, Akbar, Mahatma Gandhi, Tilak, Rabindranath Tagore, Gokhale, Bhagat Singh, Jawahar Lal Nehru, Jagdish Chandra Bose, Ramanujan, Lata Mangeshkar, Satyajit Ray and Kapil Dev. They conjure the image of India and provide inspiration to the younger generation. However, India cannot just live in its glorious past. We cannot escape the reality of the present and the uncertainty of the future. In a trance of idol worship, we often forget the younger generation. Many budding talents and unknown soldiers, who dedicate themselves to the nation, do not get their rightful recognition and credit. Often, the close circuit of well connected and publicity-minded people rob the credit due to unassuming and simple people. I discovered this fact after my visit to a jhuggi (hut) cluster. I became curious about the lives of street children. I met Raju who was selling *agarbattis* (incense sticks) at a traffic junction. He responded to my hand of friendship and took me to his hut. He is an orphan and lives with his uncle and other relatives. At the age of twelve he knows many vocations, like kite-making, spinning, carpentry and a bit of motor mechanics. He can pull a rickshaw and can drive a three wheeler and a *tonga* (horse cart). He knows horse riding, swimming, cooking and sewing. He works about sixteen hours a day without any break or holiday. He even saves some time to study. He can speak simple sentences in

English. He is dark and attractive. He sings and can imitate film actors well. He is always smiling and happy. I can never imagine that an orphan boy without home, parents, school and money can be so happy, talented and hardworking. Raju is my hero. He is a symbol of millions of unprivileged, deprived and unknown children, who have been forgotten by our society. With a little care, help and direction, they can help in building the nation much more than many of us. Raju is indeed my role model.

22. TO LIVE TOGETHER

Since the beginning of human life on earth, man has always had a quest for growth and development. This is a natural tendency of man. Everyone strives towards the development of his or her mental, physical, spiritual, emotional and social worlds. Mental development is an aspect of knowledge. Physical development means having a healthy body and keeping fit. Spiritual and emotional development deal with the feelings of love, values and beliefs. An important aspect of development is man's relationship with family and society. Everyone is interdependent in a society. It is friends and relatives who give purpose to life, love and respect. Man's existence is based on these relationships. One with faith in others can have a wonderful life. A person with little faith in others is confined to his own self. Societies are wonderfully diverse yet have many common goals. They have differences of opinions, customs and religions, yet are unified. There is unity in diversity and diversity in unity. Respect for freedom of one's own faith, customs and culture is the basic need for togetherness. "People have a right to their own minds; because this earth belongs to all of us, because the time has come for all of us, to stand together to work together, to enjoy life together."

23. OUR ENVIRONMENT

The earth has a delicate ecosystem. Its balance depends on an interlinked cycle of various activities. The environment comprises of living and non-living things. Life depends upon non-living habitat that is the air, water and soil, etc. Various types of animals and plants including human beings, aquatic life, microorganisms are interdependent on each other. Green plants are the producers. Animals as consumers, survive on them. Plants provide us food, raw materials for shelter, clothing and also clean air. They also articulate rainfall and climate. Therefore, if the greenery is destroyed, it would disturb the whole food chain and the balance in the environment. Unfortunately, short-sighted and indiscriminate industrialisation, deforestation, automation and artificial

way of life have polluted and damaged the environment in the recent past. There is a need to protect our environment by adopting an approach for development and lifestyle which is compatible with nature. The non-living things of the environment, which consist of land, rivers, oceans, lakes, air, minerals, etc., provide us resources and a suitable habitat. These are complementary to living things and are necessary for their survival. Vegetation and forests regulate climate and environment. For example, growth of plants depends upon the quality of soil, water and air. As such, it is essential that all care should be taken to maintain environmental balance and protect it from pollution.

PART – III

ESSAY WRITING

1. MAHATMA GANDHI, THE FATHER OF THE NATION

Mahatma Gandhi is called the 'Father of the Nation'. He was one of the greatest leaders of the world in the twentieth century. Due to his untiring efforts, India gained independence from British rule. His weapons in this war were unique, namely, truth and non-violence.

Mohandas Karamchand Gandhi was born on 2nd October, 1869 in Porbandar in Gujarat. His father was *Dewan* in Rajkot state. After passing his mariculation in 1887, he went to England to study law. In 1893 he went to South Africa. There he was appalled by the pathetic condition of coloured people and discrimination against the Indians and South Africans. He fought for their rights. He adopted a new method to fight against the British rulers. He practiced peaceful resistance to racial discrimination. His weapons were 'Satyagraha' (truth) and 'Ahimsa' (non-violence). After winning the battle in South Africa, he returned to India in 1916.

His aim was to gain independence for the country and build it as a self-reliant nation. He started non-violence and non-cooperation movements to achieve these objectives. He moved the masses with his sincerity, simplicity and determination. Along with many leaders and countrymen, he was sent to jail several times. Ultimately, the British realised that they could not continue to rule India. They were unable to control the fire of independence burning in the hearts of the masses. Millions were following the path of Mahatma Gandhi. At his behest, they were ready to lay down their lives for the freedom of the country.

On 15th August, 1947, the British had to retreat and India was declared a free country. But unfortunately, the country was divided into two nations, India and Pakistan. The scene after independence was terrible. There was turmoil, chaos, terror and bloodshed all over. It caused heavy loss of life, character and property on both sides of the man-made border. Gandhi was saddened by the communal hatred. He began a fast unto death, unless the conditions at Noakhali in East Bengal (now Bangladesh), which was worst affected, was brought under control. Ultimately peace returned among the Hindus and Muslims.

What Gandhi achieved in his life was a miracle. He lives in the hearts of millions of Indians and is respected by all. He laid great emphasis on banishing untouchability, promoting Hindu-Muslim unity, removal of illiteracy, development of cottage and handloom industries, equality to women and development of villages and agriculture. He believed that purity of soul could be brought by sacrifice and service to the poor. He practised what he preached. He dedicated all his life to the upliftment of the poor. He personified the principle of simple living and high thinking. He laid down his life for the country.

On 30th January, 1948, the world lost a great leader. Mahatma Gandhi was killed by a person who did not like his policies. There was gloom all over the nation. He was cremated at Rajghat in Delhi.

Although he is no more, his name lives on. He lives in the hearts of millions. Even after decades, his principles, dedication and mission continue to inspire the country. The nation will always remain indebted to Mahatma Gandhi for giving it freedom.

2. PANDIT JAWAHAR LAL NEHRU

Pandit Jawahar Lal Nehru was the first prime minister of India. He worked hard with Mahatma Gandhi in the freedom struggle. Invariably wearing a red rose, he was adored by the masses. He was a great leader and master builder of modern India. That is why he is called the 'Architect of the Nation'. He had plans to build a great and strong India. He was a man with determination and strength of character. His love of people and affection for children made him very popular. He was a great writer and thinker. He wrote the famous book, 'The Discovery of India'.

Jawahar Lal Nehru was born on 14th November, 1889 in Allahabad. His father Moti Lal Nehru was a famous barrister. He took his primary education from English tutors at home. He was sent to England for high school study. He took up his education in law. After doing law, he returned to India. He had a burning passion for his country and its independence.

He was deeply influenced by Mahatma Gandhi. His greatest desire was to see India free. Under the guidance of Mahatma Gandhi, Jawahar Lal Nehru took an active part in the freedom movement. He also followed the path of truth and non-violence. He was sent to jail many times. He was elected president of the Indian National Congress in 1929. There the pledge of independence was taken. He said at the constituent assembly, "Whether we are men and women of history or not, India is a country of destiny."

When India attained freedom in August 1947, he became the first prime minister of the independent India. His leadership and vision brought progress, prosperity and respect to the country. He laid the foundation of democracy. He believed in the principles of peaceful co-existence. In 1961, the Panchsheel Agreement was signed between India and China. He was a great propagator of disarmament. India got due respect from the world under his leadership. He worked hard to create an international order of peace and brotherhood. He followed the path blazed by Buddha, Christ and Nanak.

After serving the nation and mankind for a long time, he gained eternity on 27th May, 1964. He left behind the heritage of planning and development. He started the cycle of progress and social justice. He created a network of educational, technical and medical institutions. He built large industrial, agricultural, irrigation and power projects.

His contribution has been immense. He was one of the few men who could move the country and the world. His birthday, 14th November, is celebrated as Children's Day. This reminds us of his great character, ideals and deeds. In the words of Winston Churchill, "He had conquered all things including fear."

Jawahar Lal Nehru had a profound vision. He was a great orator and an author of repute. He believed in the unity of the country and liberty of the mankind.

3. THE INDEPENDENCE DAY

15th August is a historical day for India. It is our Independence Day. On this day, after a long and hard struggle, India won freedom from the clutches of the British rule. It was a tough war which was led by great leaders like Mahatma Gandhi, Jawahar Lal Nehru, Subhash Chandra Bose, Gokhale, Lala Lajpat Rai, Tilak, Sardar Patel and Bhagat Singh. It was a mass movement in which common people took an active part. It was the result of the sacrifice of selfless leaders and people, who dedicated their lives for future generations.

On 15th August, 1947, the nation celebrated its first Independence Day. It was a day of rejoicing and pride. Our first prime minister, Jawahar Lal Nehru, hoisted the national flag from the ramparts of the Red Fort in Delhi. This was the dawn of a new era. It was a promise of progress and prosperity.

Since then, Independence Day is celebrated every year all over the country. On this day, the sky is filled with tricolour flags. Like thousands of rainbows, flags fly in

the sky over lofty buildings. All institutions, schools, offices and colleges celebrate the flag hoisting ceremony.

The schools organise special assemblies in which homage is paid to those who laid down their lives for the independence of the country. Patriotic songs and re-enactment of famous episodes of the independence struggle are performed. These motivate children to serve the nation and be ready to sacrifice. Painting, dance, music and drama competitions are organised to commemorate the occasion. Newspapers publish special supplements on Independence Day.

Independence Day reminds us of the dedication, suffering and struggle of our freedom fighters and leaders. It is our duty to protect the freedom of the country. For this, we should remain united and work for the progress of the country. This day should not be just a ritual, but we should think of the poor who are still not free from poverty, hunger and slavery. Freedom should bring cheer to every Indian, whether poor or rich.

4. THE REPUBLIC DAY

India is a republic. This means that the people are the rulers of the nation. We are lucky to have no more kings, queens and tyrants. The rights of the Indian people are safeguarded by the constitution. This was adopted on 26th Janaury, 1950. We celebrate this day every year as the Republic Day.

The Republic Day parade on Rajpath in Delhi is a grand and most spectacular show. Every year, millions of people watch this interesting parade. It is full of folk dances, music and an impressive display of the military and its machines. School children present colourful P.T., and dances. Tableaux from various states of India display their special cultural features.

The helicopters shower flowers on the public. The fighter planes demonstrate their speed and acrobatics. The president of India takes the salute. The most important

government buildings like Rashtrapati Bhavan, Secretariat building, offices of several ministries, Parliament of India are lighted in the evening. It presents a very beautiful scene. The celebration concludes after three days at the Vijay Chowk, with 'Beating the Retreat' ceremony.

5. DEMOCRACY

Democracy is the most common form of government in the world. It literally means the 'government of the Demos'. The Demos were ancient Greek people who freed themselves from the rule of hereditary monarchs. They were the founders of this system of government. They ousted the oligarchs and established the rule of citizens. Since then democracy has evolved through the ages. It was given a new meaning by the American President Abraham Lincoln, who called it "the government of the people, by the people and for people." It opened a new chapter in the governance of a country, state, people and the world.

The cornerstones of democracy are the canons of freedom and equality. People have the right to vote and elect their own government. The government can be impeached or criticised, if it is felt that it is not working properly. Democracy provides the people with equal rights and they cannot be discriminated against on the basis of religion, caste, creed, race, colour, gender, etc. Also, all citizens have an equal right to clect and gct elected. The citizens are responsible to the government. Simultaneously, the government is also responsible to the citizens in a democracy. The government has to work for social welfare and cannot suppress the citizens. Development with social justice is the primary motto of democracy.

6. MY CITY

Delhi is my city. It is like a legend. It has many monuments representing various phases of its long history. It has been the seat of many empires. Delhi is made of seven historical cities. These cities are:

1. Mehrauli
2. Sri Fort
3. Tughlaqabad
4. Jahanpanah
5. Kotla Feroz Shah
6. Purana Qila (Sher Shah's city)
7. Shahjahanabad (Old Delhi)

The British built their capital at Raisina in 1912, which is called New Delhi. It has the President's House, Connaught Place, Parliament, Secretariats, India Gate, Central Vista and numerous gardens. Its architect was Sir Edwin Lutyens. After independence, many colonies were developed in and around the seven historical cities of Delhi.

The population of Delhi is about 12.30 millions. It is the largest city in India in terms of land area. It covers a vast area of about 1,485 square kilometres. It is the capital of the country. The Ridge is the forest in the midst of the city. It is called the 'lungs of the city'. Delhi has many large markets, like Connaught Place, Chandni Chowk and Karol Bagh. It has many colleges, hospitals, schools, temples, mosques, malls and clubs. People of all religions, caste and colour live here without discrimination. It has the largest number of cars in the country. It has embassies of almost every country of the world.

Emperor Shah Jahan, like many others, loved Delhi. He wrote the following inscription on the wall of the Diwan-i-Khas at the Red Fort:

"If there be a paradise on earth, it is this, it is this, it is this."

Living in Delhi may not be like living in paradise, but it is a privilege to live in the capital of the largest democracy of the world.

7. THE EARTH AND ITS ENVIRONMENT

Our earth is a unique planet in the universe. It is the only known planet to have life on it. Mother earth provides us with water, air and land. In other words, it provides the essential spheres of life, that is, hydrosphere, lithosphere and atmosphere. The narrow zone where the three spheres coincide, is the only life sustaining part of the earth and the known universe. This is called the 'biosphere'. The hydrosphere, lithosphere, atmosphere and the biosphere together form the surroundings of everything and is known as the environment. The earth and its environment give way to life in a variety of forms—from the microscopic and simple bacteria to the blue whale and complex human beings. A particular organism is suited to a particular place and the environment, where it can flourish, breed and survive. This place is called habitat or microhabitat.

The earth has a delicate ecosystem. Its environment is made up of both the non-living and living. The non-living or physical components are land, air, water, sun, etc., and the living components are the flora, fauna and microorganisms. Life depends on the non-living part of the earth. There is a sensitive balance between both the living and non-living and plants and animals. This balance depends on an inter-linked cycle of various activities. Thus, disturbing any one disturbs the others also. Pollution of physical components of nature will destroy life, and destruction of wildlife will ultimately destroy man.

With an ever-increasing level of consumption, man is exploding the natural resources beyond proportions and causing irreversible environmental degradation and contamination. Mahatma Gandhi had hit the bull's eye when he said, "Mother earth has enough for everyone's need, but not for everyone's greed."

Man's greed and shortsightedness have led to indiscriminate industrailisation, deforestation, over-automation, and artificial ways of living. These have polluted and severely damaged the environment. To regain the balance of the earth's ecosystem, it is necessary to reorient the prevalent ways of living, industry and transport. The development has to be environment friendly and sustainable. This is not just the best way, it is the only way; a "no choice" situation. The fight against pollution cannot be left to the government. It will be impossible to fight against pollution unless it becomes a mass movement and is considered an individual responsibility.

This can be possible through a multifarious strategy of prevention and cure, precaution and action.

8. THE FESTIVAL OF HOLI

Holi is a festival of colours, joy and fun. It is one of the most popular festivals of India. It marks the beginning of a new season. The farmers begin to make preparations to reap their crops. Holi is celebrated on the last full moon night of the *Phalguna* month of the Hindu lunar calendar.

Holi symbolises the dawn of a new season and victory of good over evil. It is named after Holika, the sister of King Hiranya Kashyap, who was a non-believer in God. His son Prahalad was a devotee of God. Hiranya Kashyap did not like the ways of his son and forbade him to worship God. When he could not control his son's devotion, he tried to kill him. Ultimately, he asked his sister, who had a boon that she would not get burnt, to take Prahalad in her lap and sit on a burning pyre. Holika was burnt but nothing happened to Prahalad. This is a popular legend, which is said to be the origin of the festival of holi.

Holi is celebrated all over the country. On the eve of holi, bonfires are lit. People worship, sing and dance around the bonfire. On the day of holi, people visit their near and dear ones. They embrace each other and forgive and forget differences, if any. They play with colours and put *gulal*—a coloured powder—on each other's forehead and face. Sweets are distributed. Noisy and colourful processions are taken out. People dance to the beat of drums. They share jokes, poetry, songs and enjoy music and dance. Children use colour-filled balloons, buckets and water pumps to throw colours on each other. It is a day filled with fun and frolic, colour and humour.

Sometimes this festival takes an ugly turn. It becomes a matter of irritation when someone uses paint, mud, coal-tar, etc. in place of coloured water. Sometimes water balloons are thrown to hurt others, and boys misbehave with girls or tease them. It becomes worse when when people get intoxicated and lose control. It spoils the atmosphere of happiness, congeniality and dignity. Care should be taken to maintain the spirit and purpose of the festival. It should be a festival of enjoyment for all. One loses the fun, if it is at the cost of others.

9. MY WINTER VACATIONS

Like the Chinese 'Yin and Yang' life is composed of opposites. Day and night, dawn and dusk, good and bad, old and young, male and female, hard and soft, work and rest, war and peace, sweet and bitter, and fun and fury are all complementary phenomena of life's cycle. The longing for a time of fun and frolic after my half-yearly examinations was obviously too strong.

And why not? After all, the winter vacations fall during christmas and the festive new year, when everybody is in a mood for fun and frolic. So, this year we planned to celebrate the new year and christmas far from Delhi, to a distant place. We went to Bangalore, the Garden City of the south, known for its charming gardens, fine climate gentle people.

It seemed that the whole of Bangalore was out to celebrate christmas and to welcome the new year.

The streets were filled with people of all sorts. Buildings and shops were beautifully decorated with colourful banners, stars etc. Many shop windows displayed the winter scene, with snow-covered christmas tree and Santa Claus on his sledge. There were many stalls selling cakes, toffees, chocolates, new year cards and decoration items.

Suddenly, we heard christmas carols and the sound of music. Boys and girls were dancing and Santa Claus, seven dwarf, teddy bear and many other fancy dressed people were distributing sweets, toffees and gifts. The crowd mingled with the dancers and started singing, dancing and rejoicing. Children surrounded Santa Claus and shook hands with him. The fancy dressed bear, elephants and hippopotamus looked funny. There was Mary with her newly born Jesus. They were surrounded by the reverends and sheep. Bright stars were shining in the sky. There were real horses, elephants and camels to give free rides to children. There was a lucky draw where everybody was trying their luck.

The not so young were surrounding the parrot astrologer, who would choose a card to tell their fortune.

There was an aquarium full of goldfish and a waterfall dropping from a miniature mountain. Chaat stalls too were crowded. Many people were enjoying the feast of fast foods.

We celebrated our new year with equal fervour in Bangalore on 31st December with midnight approaching, boys and girls, old and young all were participating in fun and frolic. The band started playing a Michael Jackson tune and everybody was thrilled. There were loud and spontaneous shrieks when a look alike of Michael Jackson came on the stage. It was hard to believe that he was not the real Jackson. He pulled me up on stage and I, with many girls and boys, started dancing and singing. No one noticed how time passed and it was only five minutes to the new year. As the clock started ringing, there was a loud blast of crackers, bombs and prinking of balloons. Everyone was wishing a happy new year to each other. After a while the music stopped and it was time to leave. We came back to our hotel. It had been a memorable time. Thus, my winter vocation was full of festive fun and frolic.

10. POLLUTION AND ITS PREVENTIONS

Pollution refers to the contamination of air, water, soil or any such unnatural disturbance in any natural element. Pollution is broadly categorised into four kinds—air pollution, water pollution, land pollution and noise pollution.

What causes pollution? Industrial waste, vehicular smoke, domestic inlet of sanitation into rivers, deforestation, etc. causes pollution. Pollution is a threat to both our health and our very existence on earth.

Air pollution refers to contamination of air due to increased emission of harmful gases like greenhouse gases, CFCs, dust, etc. Air pollution causes ozone depletion, increase in greenhouse effect leading to global warming, disturbance in seasons cycle, respiratory diseases, etc.

Contamination of water due to harmful subsances like chemicals, domestic waste, etc. is called water pollution. Water pollution causes various diseases and also adversely effects growth patterns of flora and fauna.

Soil or land pollution refers to contamination of soil due to dumping of harmful substances like non-biodegradable substances on land. Soil pollution barrens the land and the soil losses it vegetative value.

Noise pollution refers to increase in tolerable noise levels. Noise levels increases due to increase in noise created by industries, traffic, weddings processions, rallies, fireworks, etc. Noise pollution leads to hearing disorders and lack of concentration, etc.

There are various preventive measures to control pollution. To list a few, using ecofriendly substitutes like jute, cotton, CNG, etc., car pooling, relocation of industries to industrial areas, filtering human waste before letting it into rivers, dumping biodegradable and non-biodegradable waste in segregated ways to avoid land pollution, filtering industrial waste before letting it into rivers, restriction on use of harmful substances like plastics, fireworks, controlled use of fossil fuels.

There is no dearth of the methods of preventing pollution, but what is needed is our active implementation of any or all of these methods.

It's high time that we wake up and do our best to make our lives healthy and our existence long lasting.

11. A COLD SNOWY MORNING

I usually get up early in the morning. But that day I was terribly upset when my brother woke me up. It was an extremely cold winter morning. It was a torture to get out of the cosy bed. But I remember that it was not Delhi but Mussoorie, where we had especially come for a holiday. I had no choice because I had myself insisted and prevailed upon my parents to bring me to Mussoorie to see the snowfall.

Outside it was all foggy and there was hardly any trace of the sun. It was extremely cold and perhaps the coldest day of the year. After having a quick wash and breakfast, we went out of the hotel. The excitement of seeing snow made me forget the torture of the severe cold.

Lo and behold, I was thrilled to see the white landscape for the first time in my life. It was snow all around. The roofs of houses, trees, the mountain peaks and the streets, everything was covered and painted white with snowfall. I started running and jumping in excitement. I scooped up snow, made balls and started playing with them, throwing them here and there.

I made a snowman and put my hat and muffler on it. I made its eyes by inserting marbles in its face. It was a beautiful creation. When I was tired of playing, I made a painting of the scenery.

Suddenly the fog started clearing. It became warm and the people, who were shivering with cold, welcomed the sun. But I did not like it very much as it started melting the snow and destroying my snowman. When I returned after my meals, the landscape had changed completely. Ugly tin roofs started staring at us. Snow was visible only on the distant hills and the Himalayan ranges.

It was time to return and we started back. On the way, I was thinking that this was perhaps the most lovely winter morning I had experienced.

12. THE HOLIDAYS

Perhaps the most exciting word in the vocabulary of a student is 'holiday'. It gives everyone a sense of relief and freedom from work and study. Holidays go back to historic times. People in the early days worshipped the forces of nature, such as Moon, Sun, Rain, Air, Thunder and Lightning. They held frequent ceremonies and celebrations. Eventually these celebrations became yearly events. Many of the first holidays had religious overtones. They were 'holydays'. Later, when countries were formed, people began to celebrate national holidays, such as Independence Day, Republic Day or the birthday of political leaders and celebrities. Apart from these, one holiday found just about everywhere in the world is the weekly rest day. This holidays goes back to Biblical times. The book of Genesis tells that, "God blessed the seventh day and hollowed it, because on it God rested from all his work which he had done in creation."

Holidays serve an important purpose. They unite people in a common activity. It might be a prayer or a patriotic display, or just having a good time. Holidays strengthen a person's feelings towards his fellow men and women.They help to rejuvenate a tired body and mind.

In India, people follow several religions. Therefore, there are large number of festivals and holidays. These include diwali, dushehra, holi, christmas, eid, raksha bandhan, janmasthmi, Mahavir jayanti, etc. The Independence Day, Republic Day and Gandhi jayanti are national holidays. There are also state and regional holidays, which are celebrated in particular regions. Pongal, onam, Ganesh chaturthi, etc. are some such holidays.

Nowadays, many countries have two holidays per week, i.e., Saturday and Sunday. In some properous western countries there are even three holidays per week. As such people have more free time. As a result, recreational activities, travel, tourism, leisure and sports are emerging as major business and industry.

13. KITE FLYING – A SPORT

The oldest form of aircraft is the kite. It originated in China about 3000 years ago. During the Han dynasty

(2000 B.C. to 200 A.D.), the Chinese military used to attach bomboo pipes to the kite. The passing of wind through the pipes produced a whistling sound which caused enemy troops to panic and flee.

The name "kite" comes from the graceful and soaring bird, the kite. Kites can be made from paper, light wood, leaves, cloth and other materials such as synthetics, plastics, nylon, fibreglass, etc. Bamboo, light wood, aluminium and reeds can be used for making the frame. For making of the string or line (*manja*), cotton is most suitable, though nylon and polyester can also be used. Most popuparly, kites are flown for recreational purposes. However, these are also used for scientific research and for military purposes. Recently, there is a revival of kite festivals all over. One can see fascinating designs of colourful kites of various shapes and sizes during such fastivals. China, Japan, India, Pakistan and Thailand have such festivals, though these are also becoming popular in

the western countries. These have led to innovations in the design of kites like the box kite, bowed kite, parafoil kite, dragon and animals kite. Kite lovers have established clubs and organise competitions.

It is interesting to know how kites fly. The forces of lift, drag and gravity combine to keep a kite in the air. A kite must be flown in such a way that its angle against the wind, called the angle of attack, provides maximum lift to overcome both drag and gravity. The angle of attack can be controlled by one or more short lines called the bridles.

In India, kite flying is truly a sport for many. It is quite inexpensive and one does not have to depend upon anything special—playfields or even a team to enjoy it. Like the free flight of one's imagination, dreams, aspirations and ambition, kite flying gives a release to the instinctive desire to fly high in the sky.

14. VISIT TO THE ZOO

We were excited when our teacher announced that our class will be taken to the zoo. I was very keen as I love birds and animals. They are our partners. I think man would be lonely without them.

All the students rushed to the bus and requested the bus driver to take us quickly to the zoo. Soon we reached the Delhi Zoo. It is one of the largest zoos in the country. It covers a vast area of about 35 acres. It is situated near the Old Fort (Purana Qila) and is a place of great attraction. It is always crowded with thousands of people and children visiting every day. It is a beautiful place, having many kinds of trees, plants, bushes and grassy grounds. There are many animals and birds, which have

been brought from other countries. We saw beautiful birds with multi-coloured feathers. There were pelicans, Siberian cranes, peacocks, cockatoos, peahens, sparrows, nightgales, kingfishers, etc. We saw cranes, stroks, ducks, and swans swimming in the pond. Some birds were singing, chirping and whistling. We were very amused to see various kinds of monkeys, gorillas and baboons. I was delighted to see my favourite animals, which included tigers, lions, leopards and the cheetah. There were also many elephants, giraffes, rinoceros, hippopotamus and crocodiles in the zoo. The other attractions were stags, deer, hares, antelopes and rabbits. They were showing various tricks and we all enjoyed their acrobtics. It was a thrill to see lovely golden fishes swimming in the water.

After seeing the zoo, we felt tired and hungry. We sat under a tree and had our lunch. After some time, we returned to our school. We learnt many things about the animals. I saw some animals for the first time, which I had seen earlier only in pictures.

15. DINOSAURS

The film 'Jurassic park' created a storm. It evoked an interest in the earliest inhabitants of earth. It created a new hero for the children: 'The Dinosaur'. There is a craze to discover these interesting creatures who are now extinct. Dinosaurs were the forerunners of animal life on earth. Nearly 150 million years ago, the great dinosaurs ruled the earth. Dinosaurs literally means 'a terrible lizard'. Like lizards, dinosaurs had hard, rough, and scaly skins. They were cold blooded reptiles. They laid eggs and had long legs. They lived on swamps, on land, mountains, rivers, forests, everywhere on the earth.

There were many types of dinosaurs. They are divided into Ornithiscahians such as Proteceratops and had hip bone similar to birds and Saurischians with hip bone similar to lizards like Diplodocus. Some were meat eaters and others ate plants.

Dinosaurs varied greatly in their size, shape, and features. They did not live at the same time. Some lived 200 million years ago, others 70 million years ago. Not all dinosaurs were giants. Some such as Compsognathus were of the size of chicken and Heterodonatesaurus was of the size of a large dog. Brontosaurs and Diplodocus were really huge.

About 65 million years ago, long before man came

into existence, dinosaurs and the flying and swimming reptiles died suddenly. The only records left are their fossils. The reason for their abrupt disappearance is still a mystery.

16. ANIMAL WELFARE

"I can't abide a butcher,
I can't abide his meat,
The ugliest shop of all is his,
The ugliest in the street."

—Walter de la Mare

When we talk about animal welfare, the first question which comes to mind is why we need animal welfare. A friend of mine gave an interesting reply, saying it is necessary because animals provide us milk and meat as food and skin for shoes. Another said that animals provide us amusement and we should save them. Yet another friend argued that in our country, which has the largest cattlestock in the world, animals are very useful in agriculture and transport. They provide us with jobs, food and income. Another friend feels that animals welfare is necessary because as human beings, we should have compassion and sympathy towards all creatures. As animals are useful to us we have a duty to care for them. It is a pity that often animals are not provided with enough food, shelter, medical care and hygenic conditions. They are very often exploited and overloaded for economic gains. Many men do not pause for a moment while killing animals for sport and amusement. There may be various viewpoints, but it is certain that animal welfare is necessary for ecological balance and in maintaining the natural food chain. Animals are integral to our living world and environment. Like human beings, the earth is their habitat and, like us they have a right to live. It is our duty to protect animals and their welfare should be our concern. Animal wefare is not just the responsibility of the governments and organisations, but needs the participation of everyone. Traditionally, the rules for animal welfare had been a part of our religion. Every religion in India preaches non-violence and protection of animals. But during recent times, it is sad to see that we are losing respect for the rights of animals to live. Man has been ruthless and cruel towards animals. Hunting has been a popular sport, which results in loss of life of innocent animals. There are laws and regulations which control hunting and cruelty towards animals. They are not sufficient. There is a need for a public movement and change in our attitude towards the animals. We need to have a heart full of love for animals if we really want animal welfare.

Mahatma Gandhi, all his life, carried forward the message of non-violence and love for animals. This has been our heritage and soul of all the religions—Hinduism, Jainism and Buddhism.

Whenever we see an animal, let us remember the message of Lord Mahavira:

"Live and Let live."

17. A SCENE AT THE RAILWAY CROSSING

Traffic jams have become the order of the day. These are common features in prime areas of Delhi. To escape congestion and pollution, we were on our way to Badhkal lake last Sunday. It was quite unexpected to see a traffic jam in the suburbs of Delhi. There was a stream of buses, cars and trucks. Scooters and bikes were trying to squeeze through stranded traffic. Bumper-to-bumper, vehicles were literally inching forward, into whatever space available. The loud and continuous honking of horns made the whole scene utterly chaotic. The street hawkers gave a finishing touch to the scene. One could choose from cut-fruit, salad, chana, pan, chaat, tea, cold drinks and many other eatables.

I was wondering what had happened. Had there been a major accident? But everyone was looking impatiently towards their right. What was it? I got down from my car and walked forward. Oh, it was a railway crossing! The gates were closed for the train to pass. Some were eagerly looking at the signal; some were looking at smoke from the railway engine in the far horizon. A few people were inquiring from the gateman: "At what time will train come?" "Which train is passing?" etc., Wait, the train is here. It was streaming like a long serpent on the breast of earth. Its subtle curvature, sound, whistle, people standing in the doorways all remind of a typical film scene. What a beautiful scene! I started counting its bogies. There were sixty-four. I also noted the time taken by it to cross the gate. It was just sixteen seconds. This was good material for a quiz. I asked my friends what is the length of a train if sixty-four bogies cross a gate in 16 seconds at 32 km per hour. No one could tell me.

After a few minutes, the train passed and the gateman opened the gates. It was like opening the floodgates. The traffic started rushing and gushing like a flood. Within minutes the traffic cleared. It again looked like a deserted place, as if nothing had happened. We also started our engine and went to Badhkal lake.

That day I enjoyed the scene at the railway crossing more than the picnic.

18. VISIT TO AN EXHIBITION

Delhi is a place where many exhibitions are held every now and then. The largest venue of national and international exhibitions is the Pragati Maidan on Mathura Road. The India International Trade Fair is held every year during November. I visited this exhibition for the first time recently.

My first impression was that the whole place looked like fairyland. The exhibition grounds with bright colours, fountains and lighting gave a look of a grand carnival. People with their children were in a holiday mood. They were curiously looking at the exhibits, watching open airshows, eating and purchasing. There were many stalls displaying attractive clothes, fancy items such as cut–glass, chandeliers, furniture, musical instruments, books,

clay models and household goods. The attractive display of fancy items could entice any onlooker.

Children of all age groups were flocking mainly to the amusment section, computer and electronic stalls, the toy pavilion and skating rink. They were enjoying various rides, merry-go-round, tumbling boxes, giant wheel, children's train, fighting cars and many other joys rides. In a corner, a juggler was amusing children with his clever tricks. Puppet shows, street theatre, films and fashion shows had also been organised.

One of the most interesting features of the fair was the handicrafts pavilion, where craftsmen from various parts of the country were displaying their skills. Here one could get a first-hand knowledge of the rich variety of carfts which our country possesses. It was like a miniature India.

Indeed I had an exciting time at the exhibition. It was like a panorama of the country and was very educative. It was one of my most enjoyable days.

19. HUMAN BODY

Human body is a wonderful machine. It performs several functions without rest. From birth, our body continues to work, without stopping for a second.

The main organs of the human body are lungs, heart, kidney, liver and brain. These organs, which work together are controlled by the brain. Each system carries out a major function. Digestive system, excretory system, circulatory system, muscular system etc. are all controlled by the brain. The brains gives us intelligence to use our physical and mental abilities. The body has more than

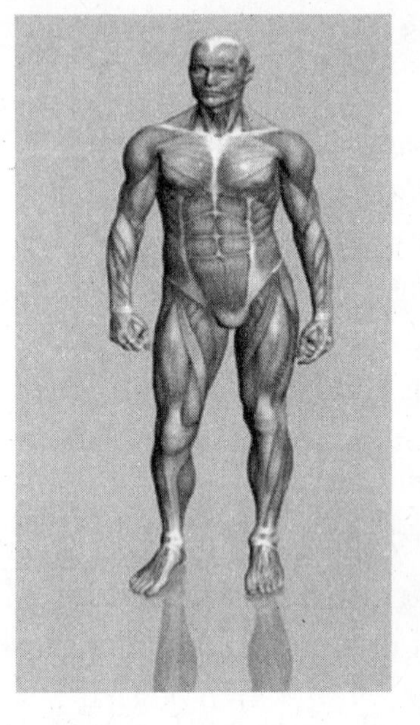

50,000 living cells of two hundred different types. These cells include neurons (nerve cells) and glands (specialised cells).

Hormones and enzymes are produced and secreted by these glands. Various types of cells perform different functions. Cells doing a similar job are grouped to form tissues. The tissues group together in a special manner to form organs.

The human body is covered by a skin. Skin is a flexible covering which protects the body. It keeps water and harmful germs out. The body's strong internal framework (skeleton) is made of 206 bones. These are connected by joints, such as in the legs. These joints help us to move. The backbone supports the head and limbs and protects the spinal cord. Between the skeleton and skin there are about 650 muscles. Nerves spread from the brain to all parts of the body. They carry signals in the form of tiny electrical impulses. The sense organs, namely eyes, nose, ears, tongue and skin, pass the message to the brain through nerves. They relay the instructions from the brain to the muscles. The brain automatically controls breathing, heartbeat, digestion, etc.

The body keeps on growing. The peak of physical growth is reached at about 18 to 25 years of age. When we grow old, the skin becomes wrinkled and less elastic. The joints become innflexible, muscles loose, bones become weak. At the climax of life, the body gives up and death occurs.

The human body is the most valuable gift of God to us. A healthy body contains a healthy brain. A healthy brain constains a healthy soul. It is very important to take care of our body. For this, regular exercise, control over eating habits, cleanliness of body and discipline are essential in daily life.

20. HEALTH IS WEALTH

> *"What a piece of work is a man, how noble in reason, how infinite in faculty. In form, in moving, how expressive and admirable in action. How like an angel in apprehension. How like a God. The beauty of the world, the paragon of animals."*
>
> – ***Shakespeare***

A great miracle is man and there is nothing more wonderful than to be healthy and happy. A healthy soul resides in a healthy mind and healthy mind resides in a healthy body. This is not myth or a fantasy but a scientific fact. Scientists have stated that, in general, a healthy body has 20% more active brain cells than the unhealthy. Therefore, a healthy person leads a more active life, is more vigilant, sharp–minded, intelligent, happy and successful.

Good health is a precious gift of nature to mankind. It is like the sun, which dispels darkness and imparts happiness. It provides freshness and refreshing energy to others. A healthy person is most welcome in society.

It is our duty to maintain the wonderful and miraculous machine called the human body. It is more

versatile and complex than any other machine or living being. The primary requisite of the body is a healthy and balanced diet. Our body needs at least 2200 calories every day in the form of cereals, pulses, milk, fruits and vegetables. The food must provide essential nutrients. Sports and daily exercise are also very important as these give proper shape and physique to the body. It builds stamina and confidence and inculcates a sporting spirit. The body needs rest and recreation. Open air activities like jogging, swimming, running, playing and yoga provide active exercise and recreation. Yoga means 'total', as the name suggests is a total process. It is a unique way to shape up the body, sharpen the mind and control the senses. This traditional Indian system of exercise lays emphasis on discipline, hygiene and cleanliness as the pre-requisites. Yoga can be practiced even while working, meditating or sleeping by maintaining proper posture.

Health paves the way for success and wealth. It helps in the development of a radiant and cheerful personality. In the modern world of machines and commerce, urbanisation and pollution, tension and rush, man is losing touch with nature. He is living an artificial life with serious ailments, sickness and diseases. He is trapped between drinks, drugs, pollution and problems. It is necessary that there is an awareness and awakening for health, nature and peace.

21. EARLY TO BED AND EARLY TO RISE

Early to bed and early to rise is a good habit. Rising early has many advantages. Early in the morning our mind is fresh and the environment is clean. There are less distractions and noise. So one can concentrate on studies and do more work. A good amount of work can be completed before others even get out of bed. One becomes a gainer, as he has much more time at his disposal.

An early riser is also a healthy person. He has time to go for a walk or to exercise in fresh air. It enables a person to accumulate energy for the whole day. After a good night's sleep, the mind is fresh. It is therefore good for students to study in the morning hours, when they can absorb the maximum. Most bright students are early risers.

As compared to early risers, late risers have a definite disadvantage. They lose their prime time in sleeping and do not have enough time during the day. This affects their studies, work and health. They are deprived of the beauty of sunrise and freshness of nature. Like a sunflower or a lotus, the mind of a man blooms with dawn and wanes with sunset. If we disregard this principle of nature, we would be working against ourselves and restricting our growth.

22. THE POSTMAN AND POSTAL SERVICE

Many people in the society serve us. These include the postman, policeman, teacher, soldier, driver etc. The postman is a person who serves everywhere without any selfish motive. He brings letters, money-orders and parcels. At times, he also helps the illiterates by reading, and even writing their letters. He is a symbol of public service. The postman is the contact person between the government and the public.

The postman is a link in the complex and long chain of the postal service. He ensures that the mail is delivered at the earliest. Whether it is a remote village or a hill station, it only takes a few days for a letter to reach any part of the world.

The first postal service was started in England in 1840. The postage stamp pays for the transport and delivery of the mail. Every country has its own stamps. These are attractively printed in a range of prices. They often depict national events and famous personalities. Whenever a letter is posted in a letter box, it is collected by a postal worker. It is then taken to a sorting office. After sorting, the letters are put in sacks according to their places of address. Postal vans rush the sacks to the aeroplanes, trains, trucks or buses going to the marked place. After reaching the destination, the letters are again sorted. The postal workers sort out the letters by street, locality and house numbers.

Nowadays, machines and computers are often used for sorting out the mail. The postman of the area collects his mail and delivers it. He generally uses a bicycle for this work. The postman has to work throughout the year, many times in pelting rain, scorching sun or chilling cold. People generally have a high respect for the postman and his sense of duty.

In spite of widespread of telecommunications like internet, mobiles and fax, the postal service still remains most reliable and important means of communication.

23. THE DOCTOR

"That service is the noblest which is rendered for its own sake."

–Mahatma Gandhi

Human life on earth is full of pleasures and sorrows, ups and downs, strengths and weaknesses, and health and illness. Like day and night these happening are eventual in everyone's life. But it is a silver lining that there are noble people who work all their lives to mitigate the sufferings of others. Among them, the profession of doctors is perhaps the most respected, for service to the society.

A doctor dedicates his life to the service of the sick. He or she relieves the sufferings and pain of mankind. He cures them from disease and illiness. He strives to

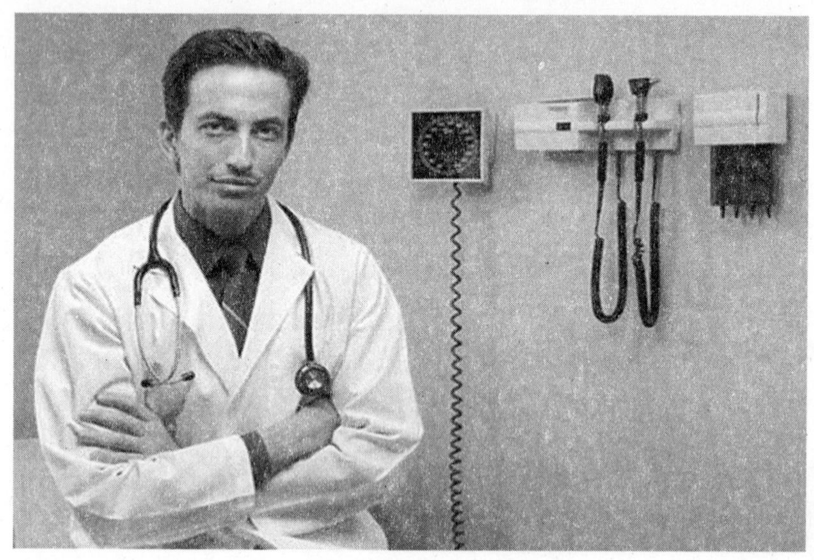

make the life of others better and healthier. The doctor works to prevent the spread of epidemics. Every now and then, new strains of dangerous diseases attack humanity. It is the doctor who finds the cure. Sometimes it may take years of painstaking work and research, but ultimately success is achieved. As a result we can see that the fields of medicine and surgery have advanced beyond imagination. Today, a damaged organ such as kidney, heart, lungs, etc., can be transplanted.

A doctor's life is hard. Often, he has to visit a patient during his off hours, forgoing his rest, sleep, and even food. Sometimes the doctor has to work day and night, attending to serious patients or victims of war, epidemic or major accident. He has to always treat his patients with a smile and cheer. He motivates and encourages sick persons. He is a source of hope and strength. Even in distress his duty is first towards his patient. Always remembering the famous Hippocratic Oath, he pledges his life in alleviating the sufferings of patients.

India has a long tradition of service to mankind. It is ingrained in its culture and all the religions. As a result, Indian doctors are well known for their charitable attitude, dedication, hard work and personal touch. They are in great demand all over the world. Many Indian doctors are working in famous hospitals abroad. India has one of the largest reservoirs of doctors. It has about 300 medical colleges, which produce about 30,000 doctors every year. They work in the cities and villages, in large hospitals or their own clinics. In recent years there has been a great leap forward in the modernisation of our hospitals with latest equipments. This has facilitated the doctors to undertake complicated operations and treat critically ill patients with success.

Besides the Allopathic system of medicine, there are doctors who practice Ayurvedic, Unani and Homeopathic systems of medicine. Innovative practices of treatment, like the Chinese acupuncture and acupressure, Yoga and natural cure have also gained popularity in the country. There is a revived interest in these systems of treatment and many allopathic doctors combine their treatment with traditional methods, like Yoga, natural cure and Ayurveda. The whole purpose is to serve mankind and remove the pain and sufferings of patients. In this respect, society is indebted to the profession of doctors.

24. THE ARCHITECT

The dictonary meaning of architect is a "Master-builder." The word architect comes from Greek, which means a craft-worker or a builder. Architect is the "art and science" of building. The architect designs a building, which should be attractive and functional. It should be

comfortable and meet the needs of the people using it. Architecture is an old art and is found in all the cultures. It is the hallmark of beliefs, tastes, style and economy. There are many historical and modern styles of architecture all over the world. The architects have created wonders of the world like the pyramids of Egypt, Taj Mahal in Agra and the Pantheon in Athens. An English architect, Sir Edwin Lutyens designed New Delhi during 1912 to 1920. It has magnificient and beautiful buildings like India Gate and President's House. After the independence of the country, French architect Le Corbusier built Chandigarh as the new capital of Punjab. It has a beautiful Assembly Complex, Secretariat, High Court and many gardens. Internationally known Indian architect, Charles Correa has planned New Mumbai. The city is being developed with many new ideas. It has well designed housing and public buildings.

If we want to build a house, we ask an architect to

design it. We have to tell him or her about our site, needs, taste and living style. The architect designs the building taking into consideration all these factors. He keeps in mind the effects of climate, materials, economy, and environment. He prepares plans, elevations, perspectives, sections, detailed drawings and models of the building. With the help of the blue prints, construction takes place. It is ensured that it takes place according to the plans. A good architect should have a strong imagination and logical approach, ideas and knowledge of methods of construction, materials and techniques. He should have a good sense of beauty and economy.

Architecture is taught in colleges all over India. There are many women architects, besides men. An architect has to work hard. It is a fascinating profession.

25. GOOD MANNERS

"We are the leaves of a tree, and tree is all humanity. We cannot live without the others, without the tree."

–Pablo Casals

It is manners which separate man from animals. In fact, the word 'manner' is derived from 'man'. That means it is a basic trait of man. A person without manners hardly deserves to be called a human being. No one likes the company of such a person, and gradually he is isolated and becomes aloof in society.

Manners are not what you say or do under the arc light. It is the reflection of behaviour with others. Good manners are the backbone of society. They are essential for social life and individual peace and comfort. To behave, speak and act politely and in the right manner constitutes good manners. John Vance Cheney once remarked, "The soul would have no rainbow had the eyes no tears."

Sympathy, love and kindness towards fellow beings are important prerequisites for everyone. It is not enough to contain these feelings in one's heart but also to express love and respect for others. Thinking about others' feelings is great and to express them in a proper manner is even greater. This is where good manners are involved.

When someone hurts you and does not apologise, it is bad manners. One can cover up this mistake by expressing his realisation and genuinely saying, "I am sorry." In this manner one avoids bitterness, confrontation and quarrels. In other words, he becomes likeable and amicable. According to A. Gardiner, "Please and thank you are small changes with which we pay our way back as social beings." It keeps the machine of life running smoothly. Sir, madam, dear, sorry, please, excuse me, thank you, etc. are some words which should be used in daily conversation. Speak softly, sweetly, and appropriately, without hurting the feelings of others. Good manners go with action. They add charm to a man's personality. If a person is kind, courteous, polite and helpful towards others, he is liked. He commands respect from others. From what we get we can make a living; what we give, however, makes a life. Besides co-operation, sympathetic attitude and tolerance, one should be a good listener. This is a trait which is often forgotten. For this one should control and restraint himself from being talkative. Self-control and restraint are cornerstones of good manners. Good manners cannot be borrowed but are to be developed through one's own behaviour. They work like a lubricant in running life smoothly.

Good manners do not mean to be always sweet and sugary with everyone. One should be honest and give a frank opinion. However, healthy cristicism should always be sandwiched between two layers of praise.

26. FRIENDSHIP

The great Roman statesman Cicero once remarked that friendship increases happiness and diminishes misery by doubling our joy and dividing our grief. What he meant is that a true friend is so delighted in our success and happiness that he/she receives as much pleasure from it as we do ourselves. In the absence of friends, the world would be gloomy. It is no use attaining wealth, power or honour, if you are devoid of a real friend. For it is he and his approval which doubles the pleasure. Joys become more intense and permanent by sharing with a friend. Friendship is an elixir which is essential for a healthy and happy life.

It is also true that friendship diminishes our misery and troubles when a friend shares its burden. Our grief is alleviated by friendly condolence. At the time of adversity, the advice and active assistance provided by a friend works like a medicine. Where a friendless man stands alone, exposed, unprotected by blows of fortune, friendship provides a strong shield against such miseries. A friendship is without caste, creed, religion, class or status. It is a feeling of love, sharing and caring. It is a shoulder on which one can rest when burdened with sorrow.

Friendship is like an ever-flowing fountain, coming up from the bottom of the heart. It is an outgoing concern, much beyond the selfish motives. Life is like mathematics and we should:

> "Add our friends,
> Subtract our enemies,
> Multiply our joys, and
> Divide our sorrows."

27. THE TELEVISION: A BOON OR BANE?

Television is one of the most wonderful inventions of the twentieth century, which has become an indispensable part of life for people around the globe. Just at a click of a button you can see what is happening in the world. You can watch a sports event live, an opera, a film or any other favourite programme on television. Nowadays, television has become the main source of entertainment. Children, men, women and elders, all spend hours in front of the television. There is a range of channels and wide choice of different programmes besides plays, songs, films, serials and other entertainment with many sports,

music, news, business and cultural shows on the television. It is also a source of education. There are educational and scientific programmes. Even farmers can benefit by learning new and modern methods of agriculture, irrigation and about fertilisers. They can learn how to get finance from banks and cooperatives. Children become familiar with the world, cultures and the advancements of science and technology. There are special transmissions for students, through which they can teach themselves. It makes learning interesting and easy. Television shows us what is happening thousands of miles away on earth. It can also show what is happening on the moon or distance stars, million of miles away. It has brought the world to our doorstep and expanded our horizons. For today's children many happenings in foreign countries, world affairs and cultures are no longer bookish and strange phenomena.

Television is a complex and complicated machine. The television shows require the services of many performers, producers, technicians, specialists and a wide range of studios and equipment. Television cameras and microphones hanging from long metal poles, called booms, follow the performers as they move about. Two television monitors reproduce the scene as they are shot by cameras. Special light effects are created by overhead lighting and special cameras. It requires hard work even to make a simple TV programme. To make it attractive, there are many creative people, writers, stage artists, architects, photographers, designers, scriptwriters, musicians and visualisers behind each production. It is a complex and expensive affair. Their transmission becomes possible by commercial advertisements and sponsors, which subsidies their production. In this way, TV has become a big business and medium of advertisement for consumer products.

Television has been nicknamed the 'Idiot-box'. This indicates the harmful aspect of TV. It absorbs the mind of everyone and often affects essential work, study and outdoor exercise. It may also vitiate tender minds with crimes, terror or evil shown in programmes. Another criticism of TV is that it reduces social life and human interaction. Therefore, it is necessary that the TV is switched on with discrimination and choice. It can be a boon or a curse depending upon how one uses it.

28. POSITIVES AND NEGATIVES OF THE CINEMA

Man has always been fascinated by dream, fantasy, fiction and entertainment. All these come rolled into one package: cinema. This is the reason that cinema has always been so popular among masses. Whether one goes to cinema halls or not, one cannot escape it. It is omnipresent: on television, radio, newspapers, magazines and in gossip.

Film making was invented about a 100 years ago. The first real film was produced by French brothers Lumiers in 1895. In India it came slightly later. Cinema's earlier days were black and white and silent. Then it was found that series of signals like those of cassettes could be applied to one side of the roll of film. Special machines turned these signals into sound. Then started the era where voices, sound and music accompained the pictures. The introduction of colour photography and techniques such as cinerama and technirama made movies even more spectacular. Over the years, techniques for shooting a movie have changed considerably. Movie operators now use much advanced equipments, including computers.

Most movie making takes place in studios, where the scenery is built to create the proper background. Outdoor shooting is, however, also popular. Special effects like 3D animation and various tricks are often used to make them dramatic and more spectacular. After shooting, the film is edited so that various scenes can be joined together.

Cinema has become one of the most popular sources of entertainment and knowledge. It is a valuable medium of communication. It is a way of recording history, translating great books and epics into an audio-visual show and promoting music, dance and other arts. It enables recording of rare events, studying environment and nature and other fields of knowledge. Movies depict life, cultures and traditions of various countries. They also deal with human relations, moral values, history, geography and science. Thus, cinema is the mirror of the world.

Against all these qualities, movies also have a darker aspect. Quite often they propagate negative values. Movies also divert the interest of students from studies and sports to gossip, music, dance and fun. Young boys and girls are often seen spending their time, imitating their favourite stars, at cinema halls, watching television or reading film magazines.

Though we cannot deny that cinema has great educational and recreational value, care has to be taken to discourage such films which damage the moral values, education, culture and tradition of the country.

29. HUMAN RIGHTS

Every human being is born with certain basic rights, such as life, health, freedom, justice and protection against exploitation and crime. These rights are not granted by anyone or the government, but are inherent within every person, irrespective of caste, creed, colour or economic status. However, it is not uncommon to find exploitation, especially that of victims of war, prisoners, slaves, poor and illiterates. Human rights are often violated by individuals, the police, military and even governments.

Taking cognisance of this fact, and concerned with the offence at international level, the United Nations on 10th December, 1948, adopted the Universal Declaration of Human Rights. It enumerates the basic human rights, namely the right to free speech, freedom of movement, judicial rights and right to take part in governance of their country. The social and economic rights include the right to equality without any discrimination of sex, caste, creed, race or colour. Further, human rights include the right to live with dignity, the right to rest and recreation and the right of equal pay for equal work.

The main problem of human rights is their enforcement. Different countries have adopted different standards and different rights. In some societies, civil and political rights are not statutory and obligatory. The United Nations and some international voluntary agencies are actively pursuing such countries to adopt the doctrine of human rights. They raise their voice, whether it is against unjust policies, official behaviour, discrimination or injustice. The media and the press can play an important role in bringing to light suppressive and discriminating policies and actions of governments, individuals or bureaucracy. Demonstrations, strikes, public interest litigations, court cases and financial assistance are other prevalent methods to provide relief from violation of human rights.

Education, alleviation of poverty and awareness among the masses are essential to check the violation of human rights and ensure basic freedom of living, expression, justice, work and recreation. This is the basic charter of the constitution, in the implementation of which voluntary agencies, community and people have an important role to play.

30. THE CURSE OF CHILD LABOUR

India is a vast ocean of human life. It is a land of contrasts and contradictions. It has small islands of progress and prosperity within an unending desert of poverty and deprivation. One is somewhat puzzled and wonders whether even after decades of independence, is this great land of ours really free? One of the most unfortunate aspects is that the worst sufferers are the innocent children. According to an UN report about 150 million children of India, between the ages of five to fourteen years, are tied by the chains of eternal bondage of debt, servitude, or slavery. These fragile hands are not free. They are robbed of their fundamental right to childhood. These helpless victims of child slavery usually work for more than twelve hours a day, without any break or holiday. They are tortured and forced to toil. Instead of playing, laughing, dreaming and studying, they work like slaves in farms, mines, brick-kilns, roadside

dhabas, tea shops, motor garages, *bidi* and other small scale industries like glass bangles, carpets, textiles, matchsticks, fire crackers and leather goods.

They are the cheapest source of human labour, the most exploited, the most vulnerable and the most helpless. These helpless children are tortured and exploited. They are the most defenceless citizens of free India.

Laws alone are not enough to fight against this crime. Political will to implement these laws is needed. Above all, the pressure of public opinion and voluntary agencies can play a big role in their struggle. The country needs all of us to fight against this crying shame. Social activitists, public representatives, individuals and voluntary organisations are required to work and fight for the human rights of these children. The parliament, assemblies of states and the government have to be alerted and sensitised to this ruthless crime. Campaigns have to be started to demand a child labour free product. Let us pledge to "make a bond against bonded labour."

31. MY AMBITION

"Lives of great men all remind us we can make our lives sublime......."

Dreams, ambitions and aspirations are inherent part of everyone's life. To become a specialised professional, glamorous star, winning beauty peagant, getting a white collar job or a government job, setting up one's own business is everyone's dream. Whatever ambition or dream one may have, one needs to put in hard work to realise it.

I would like to be a social worker. I find this is a

field with unlimited scope and potential. Perhaps India is one country in the world, where a large segment of population needs support, guidance and motivation. They can do wonders, if they get a little love and inspiration. Unfortunately, the political representatives who are supposed to help them have, by and large, become insensitive and exploit the masses for their narrow and selfish ends. The bureaucracy often behaves like the colonial masters. Many schemes planned to help hapless people, poor tribals, children, women, remain only on paper. In this political–administrative climate, even society has become insensitive towards the deprived, dejected and underprivileged. It is often witnessed that the rich are getting richer, poor are getting poorer and powerful are getting more power. It is a vicious cycle of social, political and economic power struggle, which is ruining the lives of the poor masses. There is all-round confusion, chaos and callousness. What is worse, in spite of this awareness of the problems, there is too much talk and little action. This is time we need many Mahatma Gandhis and Mother Teresas, who can work selflessly and at the grassroots levels. I do not think I can be one of them. But certainly with all earnestness and I would be alleviating the hardships of the poor, sick and needy. Working with the people would enable me to understand the world and humanity in a better way. It would give me immense satisfaction and enhance my knowledge, creativity and imagination.

Having chosen the path, I would judiciously and thoughtfully devote my time, energy and all my means to fulfil my desire. It requires great patience, perseverance and sacrifice. My dream can only become worthy of accomplishment by staying awake and working hard. The achievement of one's objective and aim is not always smooth sailing. One cannot discover new seas unless one has the courage to lose sight of the shore. For fulfilling my ambition, I have started meeting people who are in this field. I try to understand and learn about the life of the marginalised people, especially the poor. I read a lot about the country, and its economy, people, culture and political system, so that I can develop a better understanding of the society and have a better grasp of the basic issues. This is the focus of my long range vision.

32. MY HOBBIES

Life without a hobby is like food without salt. It is a hobby which makes living interesting. It is a pursuit outside one's regular work. A hobby gives one joy and pleasure. One does not get tired of it. It is pastime and a form of relaxation. In this way, while one is learning something, he is also making good use of his time.

There are many hobbies like drawing, painting, gardening, stamp collecting, photography, reading, sewing, crafts, embroidery, knitting, cooking, pet care and coin collecting. My hobbies are gardening, stamp collecting, photography and travelling.

Gardening gives me immense pleasure. When I see seeds sown by me growing into beautiful plants and blooming flowers, it gives me a great sense of fulfilment. I enjoy tending to my plants and watering my garden every day. It gives me satisfaction and helps in keeping myself active and busy. I grow flowers and vegetables in my garden. The greenery of plants and sweet fragrance of flowers are like tonic for tired eyes and mind. In a world full of tension and pollution, it is a great relief to see beautiful flowers and lovely plants.

Another hobby which I pursue is stamp collecting. I have collected hundreds of stamps. It is a pleasure to exchange stamps. I have arranged them in six albums according to the continents. My father, who often goes abroad, helps me collect rare stamps. Each stamp has a story to tell of a distant land, new people and the history of nations. I have made many friends in India and abroad by exchanging stamps. Photography is another hobby which is dear to my heart. It gives me a thrill to capture the visual beauty of the world around me. Whenever I see a beautiful flower or a bird in my garden, I capture it in my memory through the lens of my camera and develop it myself.

Travelling is my other passion. Whenever I get an opportunity to visit a new place, whether a village, city, mountain or seaside, I never miss it. It is so thrilling to see a new place and meet different people. Whenever I travel round a new place, I take my camera and capture interesting pictures of people, buildings, monuments, bazaars. It gives me immense satisfaction and pleasure. These hobbies help me to relax and have a revived interest in monotony of everyday routined life.

33. THE WORLD OF BOOKS

"The ink of a scholor is more sacred than the blood of the martyr."

India is well known for its status as the country with the second largest population in the world. However, not many know that it ranks third in the world in the field of education. It has 249 universities, over 1000 medical, engineering and technical colleges, 3500 research institutions, 2000 degree colleges and 80,000 schools. To meet the needs of education and knowledge, Indian literature provides a wide variety and range. About 50,000 new book titles are published in the country every year. The books cover a whole gamut of subjects, including special books for children. There are books on each and every subject, like architecture, medicine, computers, humanities, general knowledge, politics, fiction, science,

psychology, fine arts, history, geography, engineering, culture, tourism, heritage and religion, etc.

Besides Hindi and English, there are books in regional languages as well. Children's books are attractively produced with coloured illustrations, visuals and in simple language. The books in a shop, library or exhibition seem like a rocket fuelled with wisdom. If peace is the bread of the nation, then knowledge is the air which we inhale. The book is everything. It sustains life. It gives the right to man to preserve as lasting memory and knowledge. It inspires peace and freedom. It shows the road of development. It is a firament of human expression and spirit.

Even in this era of video,television and internet, books continue to be the best friend of man. Books remain the primary source of ideas, education and entertainment. They are the unfading light. Wisdom flows from the pages of books. Books are immortal and have no distinction of caste, creed or colour. These are incorruptible and sincere, sturdy and loyal. Through books humanity gets to know itself. People acquire wisdom, expression, experience, immortality and the lesson of history. Books are the golden light which illuminates the path of knowledge, spirituality and self-realisation.

34. TALES AND STORIES— A STOREHOUSE OF KNOWLEDGE

Whatever be the sancity of truth, the fact is that imagination has always fascinated men, women and children. In spite of endless production of stories in modern times, ancient legends, fables and tales always remain memorable. These reign supreme in the hearts of children. Perhaps the main reason for this is that they usually overflow with imagination and fantasy. Often termed as legends and myths, these stories continue to be rated among the most interesting. These include the Mahabharata, Ramayana, Sindbad's Travels and Adventures, Arabian Nights, Panchatantra, Aesop's Fables, etc. They make children giggle and cry, laugh and weep. They touch the heart and stir feelings. They arouse curiosity and imagination. The myths and legends provide their own explanation of the natural world through the adventures of demons and devils, Gods and Goddesses. In their own peculiar way, myths tell why the wind blows and how man discovered the wonderful uses of fire. Legends explain the story of mankind through the adventures of great heroes and heroines. Many of the myths and legends with which we are most familiar, originated in the Orient (East) and ancient Greece. The people of ancient Greece gave the name 'chaos' to the newly formed earth. We still use the word 'chaos' to mean a state of great confusion. The ancient Gods emerged from chaos to give the young earth order and form. Mythology tells us a number of stories about how man came to be and when he made his first appearance. The stories in legends and myths explain the experience and feelings of man, including diseases, epidemics, wars, calamities, sorrows and death. These explain how 'hope' made mankind bear its worst problem. The myths also explain the scientific and natural phenomena, like the movement of the sun, the moon, the stars and the planets, in their own way.

All this richness, variety and beauty of legendary tales and mythological stories make them immortal. Till there is life on the earth these will survive.

35. MY FAVOURITE NOVEL

A novel is a long story, which is fondly read by people of all ages. I have read many novels, but the one which has touched my heart is 'Great Expectations'.

It is one of the most famous work of Charles Dickens. This novel is a serious and interesting experiment on human behaviour. Its theme is that affection, loyalty and conscience are more important than social advancement, wealth and class.

The story is about goodness repaid. The main characters of the story are Pip, an orphan boy and Provis, a convict. Once Pip helped the escaped convict, Provis. Provis repaid this goodness after some years when he became rich in Australia. He helped Pip by making him a gentleman and sending money for his schooling, without disclosing his identity. After several years, Provis returned to England to live with Pip and to spend his money. He planned out an escape route but due to the rivalry between two convicts, he was captured by the police and sentenced to be hanged. Provis' money was seized by the government as he broke the law by coming back to England. Thus Pip could not benefit from Provis' wealth, which he had given to him. He made his fortune in Cairo and married his love Estella.

In this novel Dickens has been trying to create an impression on the readers that goodness is more important than money. He has tried to prove that Provis was not a bad man. The circumstances and lack of money had turned him into a bad man. Provis was a better man than Pip. He remembered the small favour of Pip always and repaid it whereas after becoming a gentleman and earning money Pip forgot everyone—the convict, his sister, and even his brother-in-law, Joe.

Charles Dickness has taken parts of the story from his own life. This does not make it feel dramatic or artificial. The story is very interesting, touching, and sensational. It is written in simple language and maintains a certain flow for the convenience of readers. Everyone becomes curious about what happens next. I enjoy reading this novel.

36. SPORTS AND ACADEMICS GO HAND IN HAND

It hardly needs to be proved that academics and sports go hand in hand. This is an inseparable couple. Scientific evidence has established that sports are essential for the brain and not only for the body. As we all know, there are more than 35 million cells in the human brain, of which many are dormant and some active. The scientists have discovered that a student who is regular in sports has 20 to 25% more activated cells than a student who is not active in sports. This reinforces the age old saying that, "All work and no play makes Jack a dull boy."

Sports help a boy or a girl to develop confidence. He or she becomes capable to face the vagaries of real life. Sportsman-spirit helps a student to laugh even when he loses. Every person has to taste bitter losses and sweet wins in his life. A sportsperson can bravely face the burdens and tensions of real life.

It is a pity that some students, while trying to achieve academic success, give up a major fulfilment of their lives, that is sports. Chances are, they are neither good at academics nor successful in sports. Success will surely come to them if they strike a balance between sports and studies. They will enjoy a full life rather than becoming single-track scholars with thick spectacles and thin shoulders.

38. WHY TOURISM EDUCATION IS A MUST?

"Oh my God, not another subject!" Any student, crushed under the heavy weight of the school bag, would react so if asked, "How about a new subject on tourism education?" "But how do you feel if it means no books, no examinations, no homework, but picnics, touring, visiting forests, monuments and villages, meeting new people, trekking, mountaineering and all that?" Anybody would exclaim, "Why not!" This is what tourism education is all about. It can be the most fascinating way to understand culture, history, geography and environment. We study all this in school which is compartmentalised into separate subjects, like history, civics, social studies, geography, science and environment. Often we ask ourselves—what is the need of knowing about the dress worn by Akbar? Or, how does it matter to us if Abraham Lincoln was not tall or who killed Caesar? Often there is no interest and overall understanding of isolated subjects, but these are compulsively crammed for examinations.

Tourism education can be a practical and interesting way to know the relevance of all these subjects. It integrates theory and reality, past and present and myth and facts. It helps us to broaden our horizons and to appreciate diverse cultures, ways of life, religions and attitudes. This is necessary to develop a feeling of unity and harmony among the people of our vast subcontinent.

Tourism education at school level will be a long term investment. It is often said that children are the future of a country. If they know the country well, they can influence other people to come as tourists and help bring honour and goodwill to the country.

Tourism education can be a source of fun and recreation for a harried student life. It can provide relief from the boredom of classroom and tensions of bookish knowledge. It can indeed provide a better understanding and appreciation of various subjects taught in school.

39. A DATE WITH THE PRESIDENT OF INDIA

14th November, 2009. This was my date with the president of India. We were invited by Mrs Pratibha Devisingh Patil, the president, the first citizen and the highest authority of the land. The occasion was the children's day I was invited because I got first rank in science Olympaid and other children invited there had also achieved some or other laurel to their school and nation. We reached the *Rashtrapati Bhavan* at 10.30 am. We were received by her reception staff. A guide then showed us the entire *Rashtrapati Bhavan* and its beautiful Mughal Gardens. This is a grand building built with red Agra and Dholpur stone. It has many beautiful paintings, antique wall clocks, armours and attractive furniture. The painting that impressed me most is a mosaic made of various kind of stones. I was also impressed by the Darbar Hall, which is under the main black dome of the *Rashtrapati Bhavan*. Ashoka Hall is decorated with mirrors, wooden flooring, beautiful carpets and glass chandeliers. The guide showed us the bust of Sir Edwin Lutyens, who was the architect of the house. We also saw the attractive paintings of all the former eleven presidents of India and pictures of eminent political personalities of India like Mahatma Gandhi and Jawaharlal Nehru. We also saw the beautiful flowers blooming in the Mughal Gardens, where the cuckoos were singing.

After seeing the president's house we went to the morning room. This was the venue of the function. When the president came, my teacher presented her a bouquet. The president sat on her special chair in the middle. We sat to her side on sofas. We were introduced to the president and shook hands with her. All the guests were served with cold drinks and snacks. The president was happy to meet us and complimented us for our achievements. She asked about our school and studies. I proudly told her about my school and my studies.

After the function was over we returned home with big smiles on our faces. It was a lifetime experience to meet the honourable president of India.

40. THE COMPUTER

Perhaps the greatest invention of the twentieth century is the computer. It is a high leap forward in the field of science. A computer is an electronic brain which can perform many tasks. It is a verstile device which can compute and interpret information very quickly. It can do various tasks. These are nowadays used in almost every

field, like weather forecasting, entertainment, business, marketing, planning, design, education, publishing etc. They are even used for making films and cartoons. The famous film 'Jurassic Park' used computer graphics to create dinosaurs. Computers have become so common that these are found everywhere in schools, homes, hotels and offices. People can even be seen using portable computers, laptops, while travelling. A computer is made up of tiny electronic circuits. Every computer has a keyboard, which acts like a typewriter. The monitor is like a TV screen which we can see. There are various softwares which can be used for various programmes. According to functions, the computer processes the information. The software for games, general knowledge and graphics are very popular among children.

Computer has become an integral part of life. Without it, it would be impossible to perform many jobs. That means, without the knowledge of computers, life would be incomplete. That is why in every good school, working on computers is taught to children. I find it very exciting and interesting. The computer, indeed, is a wonder of modern science.

"Too much of anything is bad" computers are no doubt the magic button of modern science but if excessively used it can lead to serious health problems. Long hours of computers use can lead to weak eyesight, lack of concentration, lesser ability to write manually, unablity to do manual calculation, obesity. Computer games, music, movie entertainment on computer leads to the addiction of computers. Excessive use of internet can lead to less socialising and more aloofness.

If decisively used, computers can work wonders for us.

41. THE CULTURAL HERITAGE OF INDIA

India is not just land, mountains and rivers. It is not only the second most populated country of the world and seventh largest country in area. India is you and me, and all the millions of young and old, who are her citizens. The thoughts and actions of people who have inhabited India for thousands of years have moulded our society.

There is something very unique and different that has continued in India all these years. What is this something? Close your eyes and thousand pictures of exuberance will flash through your mind: its festivals, dresses, dances, rituals, religious ceremonies, music, food, lifestyle, art, sculpture and architecture.

India is a legend that lives. It is an anthology of various cultures with their never fading beauty, colour and pageantry. Steeped in history, India is like no other country in the world. Like unending layers of culture, India unveils itself to reveal its different faces and facets. In fact you can say nothing about India without the opposite being equally true.

India is unimaginably intriguing. The great mythological epics—Ramayana and Mahabharata, lost dynasties, the splendour of remains of many empires and cultures, glamour and mystique, intellectual stimulation, spiritual peace, joy of enchanting dances, artistic creations, sound of music, tingling of bells, all combine to make our culture unique.

India's culture goes back thousands of years. Not many countries in the world can claim to have descended from ancient civilisations like India.

As time winds its way through the cosmic clock, cultures fall asleep, fade or die. But Indian culture will never die.

In recent times there have been certain instances, which are scars on our cultural and communal harmony. Such incidents are the consequences of narrow-minded and fascist forces. All of us have a responsibility to honour the socio-cultural and religious sentiments of various communities of the country.

Let us take a pledge to earnestly work for national integration and cultural harmony of our great India.

42. EDUCATION IN A DEMOCRACY

Democracy means government of the people, by the people and for the people. The working of democracy depends on the capability and activities of its citizens. Education is the only way to enable a citizen to meaningfully participate in the democratic process. An educated person is able to differentiate between good and bad. He is in a better position to perform his duties and understand the rights. He is conscious, well informed and can understand the national problems. This helps him to contribute his bit in the process of development at every level; right from casting a vote for choosing the right candidate in the parliament, down to the implementation of the policies and programmes within the democratic setup of the government.

A preliminary requisite of education is literacy. It is an indicator of the progress of a nation. Achieving literacy has been one of the most difficult challenges in India. Since independence, the government has taken multipronged actions to spread literacy among the poor masses so that the country can progress.

Today our country has witnessed a revolutionary change in literacy and education. In some parts of the country like Kerala, there is nearly 100% literacy.

Likewise, programmes and campaigns have been vigorously pursued all over the country. Financial and other supports are extended to eradicate illiteracy from India. Literacy Day, Week and Year are celebrated in the country. These play important roles in making the people aware of the importance and cause of literacy and education. Special emphasis is given to make the poor, adults and rural folk, women and backward classes literate.

Adult education programmes are undertaken in night schools, so that the livelihood of such people is not affected. Various national and international voluntary organisations, which include the United Nations and Mahila Mandals have been giving support and facilities in their endeavours in this field.

Education and literacy programmes are also implemented by postal courses, radio, television and satellite programmes.

To make literacy programmes attractive, these are often conducted in local languages, through films, plays, and cultural programmes.

Literacy and education programmes are related with employment, vocational and economic opportunities. All over the country there has been an incredible growth in the number of vocational schools, colleges, universities, industrial training institutes and polytechnics. Today there are more than 80,000 secondary schools, 500 polytechnics, 5000 colleges and 249 universities in the country. To ensure educational facilities for the underprivileged, reserved seats are kept for the scheduled castes and scheduled tribes.

Under the constitution, primary education has been made free and compulsory for everyone. The government and local bodies are obliged to run primary schools in every village or locality. The country is today dotted with more than one lakh such schools, which provide free education upto primary level. The successful functioning of a democracy depends upon the level of education, which is a must for people.

43. MY SOLUTION TO INDIA'S PROBLEMS

India, today, is inundated with major problems. Newspapers, TV, radio, web portals and day-to-day conversation revolve around all sorts of problems—population, pollution, scams, poverty, unemployment, Kashmir, Ayodhya, food, health, education, discrimination, terrorism, corruption, etc. The list is unending. Karl Marx once remarked, "Religion is the opium of the masses." Today the 'problems' have replaced religion. Society makes everyone feel as a problem. It seems that India today is in the grip of a problem-psychosis more than the problems.

Many of the problems are imaginary, magnified and made complicated. For instance, the Mandal Commision to review reservation quotas. The attempted solution to the problem became a bigger problem than the problem itself. Perhaps this is also true for most of the problems, which are either generated from attempted solutions or magnified beyond proportion.

So, what is the solution? First of all, we have to change our perception. We have to understand the problems in our own social and political context. Our attitude towards the problems has to be positive and action-oriented, rather than negative and critical. We have become very fond of telling the government and others, what should be done."What can I do?", should be the approach. If all of us do our bit, most of the problems will be solved by themselves. This approach will stem bitterness and confrontation and we will be at peace with each other.

India is a vast country with millions of able, skilful, hardworking and loving people. It is very rich in resources and has tremendous potential for growth. It is unfortunate that the so called "system" is unable to harness this potential. Rather than enabling the people to do their best, the present system makes individuals feel insignificant among the one billion. There is a need to motivate and mobilise the human resources of the country to do their best. For this, is very fundamental need is to make every individual feel like an important and useful member of the society.

Education is at the heart of any solution we may think of for the problems of India. There is need to revolutionise the educational system, which should be the focus of all the efforts.

An age old Chinese proverb is very explicit in its relevance:

"If you plan for a year, plant a seed. If for ten years, plant a tree. If for hundred years, teach the people. When you sow a seed once, you will reap a single harvest. When you teach the people, you will reap a hundred harvests."

44. BUILDING MODERN INDIA THROUGH NATIONAL INTEGRATION

India is a great country. It is one of the largest countries of the world. With a population of about 1.15 billion, it is the second most populated country. It is the seventh largest country in the world, with an area of about 32,87,872 sq. kms. About 200 languages and dialects are spoken in India. Our country is divided into 28 states and 7 union territories. It is a kaleidoscope of contrasting cultures, ethnic societies and rich heritage. It is a subcontinent with vast variations in economy, cultures, languages, climate, religion, arts and crafts.

"Unity in diversity" has become one of the most

hackneyed slogans. As we talk of it, the situation of unity becomes more desperate. A close look at the situation is revealing and startling. It is a shocking fact that during the last 62 years of independence, there has been a progressive "disunity in diversity." Kashmir, Punjab, Assam, Bihar and many other states are in turmoil. Many parts of the country are in the grip of terrorists and separatists. Many areas are threatened by the demands of subdivision and autonomy. The Herculean efforts of Mahatma Gandhi and Sardar Patel brought together scattered kingdoms, states and empires within the mainstream of a united India. Today, it seems to be on the verge of collapse.

The crisis of unity is also discernible in case of other nations. Certain nations, though small and with limited resources, achieved a phenomenal level of economic growth. The so-called four tigers of Asia, viz. Hong Kong, South Korea, Singapore and Taiwan are glaring examples. On the other hand many large nations with central rule collapsed or receded.

"Divide and rule" had been a popular colonial tool and a symptom of imperial history. If it is a fact of politics, conversely "Unite and do not rule" is equally true. There is no doubt that unity and rule do not go side by side. In a democratic setup, political and bureaucratic systems have to be subservient to people and not their masters. In other words, for integration of the country, in place of centralised, dictatorial and strong government, local autonomy and self-rule are the essential prerequisities. What we mean by 'modern' is a matter of individual perception. For some, India is already in a post-modern era. Some people think that trendy wear, sports shoes, jazzy music and fast food mean modern India. The question is whether there is something wrong with the traditional India? Have the modern developments disintegrated Indians into contrasting islands of prosperity and abject poverty? In the name of economic justice and social equity, are we not creating new subdivisions of a homogeneous society? Is it a valid concept to divide the society on the basis of castes and economic status like EWS, LIG, MIG, HIG, etc? These questions are necessary to pose in order to understand the meaning of the key theme, i.e. modern India and national integration. Unless we understand these basic issues, we will continue to indulge in daydreaming.

In my view, national integration does not mean a centralised and commanding structure of government. It does not mean uniformity. Adoption of certain national attributes like language, dress or colours is a superficial concept of national integration. On the contrary, such ideas are counterproductive to unity and integration. What is required is an understanding attitude towards local context, pecularities, culture and lifestyles. National integration is a horizontal concept, whereas the vertical hierarchical structure of the government goes against its basic character. Therefore, we will have to envolve an innovative approach based on horizontal linkages, rather than perpetuating the British and colonial system where the government is the master and people are its subjects.

National integration cannot be achieved until people have control over their situations. Let them be comfortable with their own traditions. This would offer them a 'better life' within the framework of 'Modern India'. We are in a world where economic criteria and theories of social development are no longer sacrocant. If the efforts of national integration from the commanding heights have failed, can the intiative at local level achieve much?

This would be a certain way to build a modern and integrated India—the India of Mahatma Gandhi's vision.

45. HOW I WOULD REFRAME HISTORY

Since the Stone Age, history of mankind is a statement of his lust and greed, crime and punishment, progress and destruction, terror and valour, love and hate and war and peace. It is the story of emprerors and beggars, winners and losers, rich and poor, rulers and subjects and great and small. Like the never-ending tide of the sea, it is a continuous battle of ups and downs, and attacks and repulsions. Millions have been killed and billions have been exploited throughout history. The river of history has been overflowing with the blood of the innocent. There have been brief spells of unity, progress and peace. Perhaps history does not tolerate peace and prosperity. Tranquility has always been shattered by explosions of wars and weapons.

I wish I could reframe history. It may not be possible for me to change the world, but who can stop anyone from dreaming? And dreams give birth to plans. Plans generate programmes and action converts them into reality. So I have a dream and a plan to change the course of history.

The first thing I would do is to banish the military, arms and ammunition from the world. I will also banish the names of all the warriors including Genghis Khan, Temur Lang, and Hitler from the books of history.

If I had the power, I would dismantle the dominance

of the superpowers. For the purpose of global social justice and to remove hunger and poverty from the world, I would impose an international tax, to be paid by the rich countries to the poor countries. My dream is also comprised of several fantasies. I have a vision to create a new set of seven wonders of the world. These will include a space station for UFOs, a city on a planet, a city under the sea, a computerised school without books, a solar power house and a manmade ozone layer. My dream is that travelling to other planets should be as easy as travelling between Delhi and Mumbai.

My dream is to reconstitute a greater India, as it was thousands of years ago. It should again become a golden bird with many autonomous states.

I would like that the concept of government in its real sense that is service to the people rather than governance. For this, I would diminish the powers of political masters and abolish the vertical command and structure of bureaucracy. I would reserve 100% of government jobs for the underpriviledged. The struggle for power among politicians will vanish if the government becomes powerless.

The most disturbing fact is the environmental pollution. If I had my way, it would be compulsory for everyone to plant at least one tree every year. Otherwise, he would lose his or her citizenship and rights. I would create an Environmental Defence Force. Like Maharaja Ranjit Singh, who asked every family to give one person for defending the nation, I would make it compulsory for every family to give one person for the Environmental Defence Force.

We have wasted a lot of time in half–hearted reforms. Things are going from bad to worse. Without wasting any more time, it is necessary that reforms are replaced by a 'revolution'. This is the only way that history can be reframed.

46. GENDER EQUALITY

"*Sure God created man before women. But then you always make a raugh draft before the final masterpiece.*"

– ***Anonymous***

Whether or not God created women before man or vice versa, it does not give either of them a cause for domination over the other. But unfortunately ours have become a male dominating world. Ever since antiquity, women have been fighting to free themselves from male oppression. Though, times are now changing we see

women entering every walk of life but statistics still are poor. Women can be seen in every field but their number remains to countable few, like in top notch executive positions, politics or armed forces.

Trend has changed drastically in urban scenario but the picture is still gloomy in rural areas, especially in developing countries. People are still unaware that women are equal to men in every aspect, so why think them to be burden or inferior. Thus, women alike men has all equal human rights be it right to education, freedom, right to economic independence, or right to expression, etc.

We should stop stereotyping women and grant them equal rights not only on paper but in practice. It is the time we stop giving dolls to girls and bat and ball or cars to boys. Why assume that girls are physically weaker to boys? Why can't a girl play with bat and ball and a boy play with kitchen-set or a doll. This is how we assume things and start believing them and inculcate the same in all generations.

The stress of living in the modern world, combined with 'sex role' strains, creates a tragic situation for both men and women.

Gender discrimination perhaps discrimination of any kind is a setback to the unity of society and development of human resources.

It's time we accept that our delicate friends, loving mother, sister and caring wife to be our tough competitors/ colleagues, rivals and bosses.

It is high time we give full justice to half the world's population i.e. women folk and thus double our workforce and cater equal human rights. We cannot imagine our lives without women not for the fact that they give birth to us but also for the reason that they all are our equal counterparts.

47. NUCLEAR ENERGY: USES AND ABUSES

The latest discovery of science is nuclear energy. Nuclear energy was first discovered by the French physicist, Henry Bacquerel, in 1896. Nuclear energy is released by the splitting (fission) or merging together (fussion) of the nuclei (the smallest element of atom) of atom.

Nuclear technology or energy is used to produce electricity from power reactors, it is used in agriculture, medicine, industry, biology, etc.

Though presently nuclear energy is the best alternative for increasing requirement of energy, but we cannot overlook the ever-increasing misuse of nuclear energy and also the development of sophisticated, and powerful nuclear weapons. Cases like Chernobyl disaster, Hiroshima-Nagasaki and the Bhopal gas tragedy testify to the ill-effects of nuclear energy. More, recently, there is a great problem of the disposal of radioactive waste of nuclear energy process. Radioactive waste is fatal to the life of human, animals and fertility of land and purity of water. Scientist have failed to pave a way for proper disposal of radioactive waste, radioactive waste dumped anywhere near human or flora or fauna inhabitance would pose a threat to their survival. Radioactive waste is so dangerous that large quantities of it are dumped deep into Pacific Ocean, but there also it destroyed aquatic plants and animals. Now scientists are planning for space disposal of radioactive waste, wherein all radioactive waste would be loaded in a rocket and launched towards some other planet where it would not have any form of life, to be destroyed. It only tells us that how dangerous is radioactive waste for any form of life.

But nuclear energy is the most cost effective and non-polluting source of energy which is a great alternative for the ever increasing demand of energy.

Nuclear energy, like any other technology, if decisively used can prove to be a boon for us but it can turn into a bane if misused. If nuclear energy is used only for developing nuclear weapons then the life of human is sured to be doomed at hands of nuclear weapons wars. Hence, it depends entirely on us whether to cash in the uses or abuses of nuclear energy.

48. GLOBAL WARMING

The most recent and most alarming threat to the environment and human existence rather to all forms of life is 'global warming'. Global warming refers to the increase in the relative temperature of earth's surface. The temperature of earth's surface has increased 1°C in the last decade. The apparent increase in global warming is due to increase in emission of greenhouse gases likes carbon dioxidc, nitrogen and CFCs leading to increase in greenhouse effect. Greenhouse effect refers to process wherein the greenhouse gases trap the heat and infrared rays radiated back by earth's surface. The increase in trapping of infrared rays leads to an increase in temperature of earth's surface.

The emission of greenhouse gases have increased enormously due to increase in human activities like industrialisation, transportation and deforestation.

Global warming leads to various natural catastrophes like glacier melting, extreme cold and hot, disturbed seasons' cycle, excessive rains, excessive drought, floods and earthquakes. Going by present rate of increase in global warming and no control measures or remedies, the day is not left far behind when this earth would be submerged under water.

All forms of life would extinct from the face of the earth. All our technical advancement would be useless if we cease to exist.

The only control measures which can help to control or balance global warming are: control over emission of greenhouse gases and afforestation. Only a controlled check over environmental pollution can help our mother

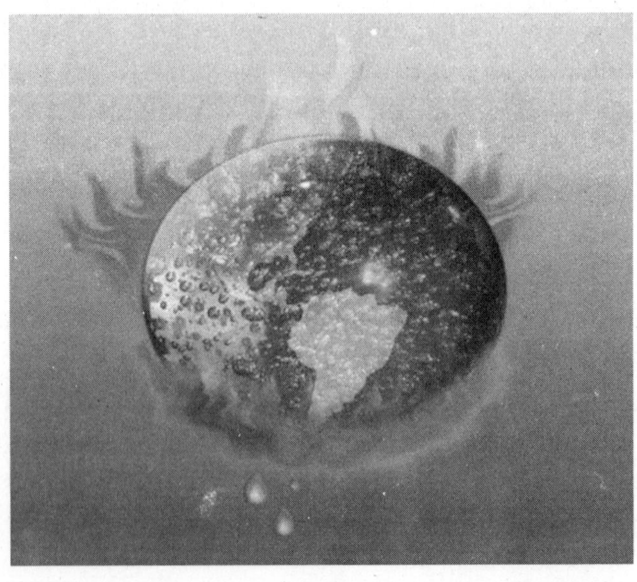

earth to cool off back to normal. Don't wait for anyone, government or NGOs to do that, do your bit to save life from extinction and secure your own future.

49. INTERNET: USES AND ABUSES

'Internet' stands for 'Inter Connected Network'. Internet is a network of millions of computer networks across the globe. 'Internet' was developed in 1960's in Department of Defence of US and was meant to share data of three computers at different locations. Gradually from military uses to education and now in commerce, trade and every field internet has gained wide popularity.

Today internet is a need of every office, home or business. Internet offers a wide range of services and facilities like data sharing, data transfer, social networks, electronic mail, live chat, live voice chat, live video transfer, tele-conferencing, e-trade, e-commerce. It can serve as a source of research for schools and scholars and

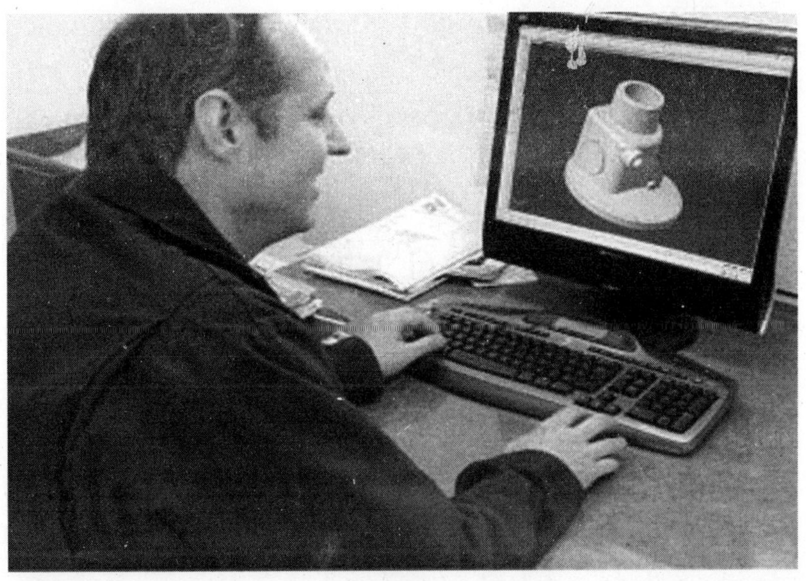

another publicity platform or medium of communication for a company. Literally internet has turned the world into a global village. Gone are the days of waiting or months on an end to receive a letter from your friend or relative, from a distant place. At click of some buttons you can talk to anybody sitting in a remote or distant part of the world, all you need is access to computer and internet at both sides.

But internet can turn into an ugly monster if used unwisely, like any other technology, internet should be used decisively.

We should avoid using internet only for excessive and useless chating and surfing. Avoid talking to remote strangers on internet who can harm us by using our personal and sensitive data. Crime over internet is called cyber crime. Some evil souls try to harm our data by emitting virus or hacking our data by hacking our sites or passwords of commercial transactions. There are hosts of websites with vulgar stuff but it is entirely our choice to avoid them.

Hence, it entirely depends on us whether to make advantageous use of internet or not. If used wisely internet can work wonders for our help and success.

50. GLOBAL TERRORISM

'Terrorism' refers to the use of violence or terror to force others to comply to one's demands or ideologies. Terrorism on a global level is termed as 'global terrorism'. Terrorist can be an individual or an organisation; anyone who uses terror as medium to force his/her conceptions or demands is called a 'terrorist'.

Terrorist does not belong to a particular community, religion, nation, caste, colour or creed but rather they are antisocial elements who choose wrong way to get their demands fulfiled or ideologies followed.

Terrorists are friends or saviour of none rather they are enemy to everyone, enemy to humanity, enemy to peace and harmony of the world. Terrorist can do good to none and solve no purpose.

Terrorism just kills and spread terror. It does not help to resolve any issues and it offers solutions to nothing. Be it 9/11 attack on America or 26/11 attack on Mumbai, the terrorist attacks may shake the world for a small time but it cannot certainly shake the faith in harmony, peace and non-violence.

Terrorism can be defeated only with stern actions

against terrorist outfits and people spreading terrorism in the disguise of religion and nationalism. Unity, peace, harmony, love, non-violence can be only answer to terrorism.

In wake of recent attacks on America and India a new wave of 'anti-terrorism actions' have started across the globe. If terrorism has gained a global level so has to be 'anti-terrorsim actions' i.e. we need to have 'global anti-terrorism actions'.

PART – IV

LETTER AND APPLICATION WRITING

FORMAL LETTERS

1. A letter inviting a school to participate in a drama competition

Delhi Public School
Mathura Road
New Delhi-110003

19th October, 20____

The Principal
Modern School
Vasant Vihar
New Delhi

Sir

Your school has always been very active in extra curricular activities. Your students have been regularly participating and winning in the G.K. Quiz, dance competitions, music competitions and other programmes. Our school, i.e. Delhi Public School, Mathura Road is organising a drama festival called the 'Dramafest'. Your school is cordially invited to participate in it. This festival is an effort to spread the message of love, peace and unity. Thus, the topic chosen is 'universal brotherhood'. The following points may please be noted:

1. The drama should be in English.

2. The time limit is 20 minutes.
3. The decision of the judges will be final.
4. Each school can perform only one drama.
5. The Dramafest will take place on 21st and 22nd January, 20__.
6. The venue will be Delhi Public School, Mathura Road, New Delhi. For any clarification, kindly contact me on phone no.: __________.

An early reply is requested. A favourable response is expected from your school.

Thanking you

Yours faithfully

Amit Tanwar
Dramafest Chairman and
Cultural Secretary

2. A letter reporting theft of a bicycle

280 Pocket C
Malviya Nagar
New Delhi

14th November, 20___

The S.H.O.
Police Station Hauz Khas
New Delhi-110003

Sub: Theft of bicycle

Sir

With due respect and confidence in your efficiency, I am

lodging a report about the theft of my bicycle on 13th November, 20___. On this unfortunate day, I went to K-71 Hauz Khas Enclave to meet my friend on my bicycle. I parked the bicycle along the wall of Hauz Khas police station. After an hour, i.e. around 4 p.m., when I returned to the spot where I had parked my bicycle, I was shocked to find that it was missing. I looked around and at a distance of about 200 mtrs, I saw a man riding it. When I shouted and raised an alarm, he got lost in the milling crowd. I immediately reported the incident to the duty constable at the police station, but he did not register my FIR. On the contrary, he accused me of parking the bicycle at the wrong place and without a proper lock. The attitude of your official is shocking and that is why I have to write to you.

The colour of my bicycle was red and it was bought recently from M/s Atlas Depot, Hauz Khas. It was Avon 747 model. Its frame number was KAV 747935 D. A photocopy of the cash receipt of the cycle is enclosed.

Although I did not see the man clearly, he was around 30 years of age, well built, tall and had long hair. He was wearing a loose jacket over a red checked shirt and black trousers.

I shall be grateful if early action is taken in finding the bicycle. I would be waiting anxiously for your call.

Thanking you

Yours faithfully

(Anuj Agarwal)

3. A letter to the general manager, D.T.C., complaining against the misbehaviour of a bus conductor

174 Tagore Park
New Delhi-110006

12th July, 20____

The General Manager
Delhi Transport Corporation
Azad Bhavan
New Delhi

Sir

I would like to bring to your notice the misbehaviour of a bus conductor. The incident took place on 10th July, 20____. I was travelling on bus number 502 from Saket to Ajmeri Gate in the morning, at about 9.45 a.m. I was going to Connaught Place. I had given him a ten rupee note to buy a ticket. But to my surprise the conductor sat lazily and did not give me the ticket. As I reminded him he started abusing and misbehaving. When I demanded the complaint book, the conductor refused to hand it over to me. Due to the intervention of follow passengers, the incident was averted from taking an ugly turn. I hope action will be taken against the conductor for his rude behaviour.

Thanking you

Yours faithfully

(Vivek Kapoor)

4. A letter reporting loss of luggage on the train

B-60 West Patel Nagar
New Delhi-110008

26th October, 20____

The Station Master
New Delhi Railway Station
New Delhi

Sub: Loss of luggage on train no. 2567 UP-Assam Express

Sir

I was travelling on 25th October, 20____ on train no. 2567 UP-Assam Express. I boarded the train at Patna, in first class A.C. compartment. It was a night journey. The train reached New Delhi at 6 o' clock in the morning. When I started to pack my belongings, I was surprised to find that bag was missing.

It was a 24" leather bag, red colour with belts. This bag has castor wheels and was fitted with extra locks. Besides my clothes and daily accessories, it contained my passport and other important documents. I have already lodged an FIR with the railway police and am writing to you kindly initiate extra efforts to find the lost luggage.

At the same time, I wish to bring to your notice that the security staff in the compartment had been sleeping. It is requested to kindly take action for their negligence towards their duty, which has caused me this loss.

Thanking you

Yours faithfully

(Arun Kumar)

5. A letter to the editor submitting an essay

180 Asian Games Village
New Delhi-110049
Tel.:________

27th March, 20_____

The Editor
Indrama
C/o Sita Travels
Connaught Place
New Delhi-110001

Sir

I am a student of Delhi Public School, Mathura Road, and had recently visited Gujarat and Diu. I have recorded my impressions and reflections in my article 'A Schoolboy's Journey to Gujarat and Diu'. Though a bit unusual, I hope that you will publish it. I can send colour photographs illustrating the article, if you decide to publish it. The article is exclusive for Indrama and unpublished.

Thanking you

Yours faithfully

(Mohit Verma)

6. A letter to the editor submitting an article

25 Sarojini Nagar
New Delhi

27th March, 20____

The Editor
The Hindustan Times
(Saturday Magazine)
New Delhi-110001

Sir

'The Earth and its Environment' is the concern of today. Its disturbing state of serious ailment prompted me to write the enclosed article for the Children's Page of the Saturday Magazine. I hope you will find it worth publishing.

If unpublished, kindly return the article.

Thanking you

Yours faithfully

(Ruchi Jha)

7. A letter submitting an essay for a competition

180 Asian Games Village
New Delhi-110049
Tel.: ________

15th March, 20_____

The Editor
Dircctorate of Adult Education
Block No.10 Jamnagar House
Shah Jahan Road
New Delhi-110001

Sub: Submission of essay for national essay competition {(a) 9-12 class}

Sir

Please find enclosed my essay on 'Literacy for Learning Society' for the national essay competition. The required details are given below:

Name	:	Nikhil Arora
Age	:	15 yrs. (D/B: 13.8.19__)
Sex	:	Male
Class	:	X
School	:	Delhi Public School Mathura Road New Delhi
Nationality	:	Indian
Res. address	:	180 Asian Games Village New Delhi-110049

Res. phone no.: ___________

CERTIFICATE

I hereby certify that the enclosed essay is my original work and has not been published in any other publication.

Yours faithfully

Nikhil Arora

8. A letter for club membership

9-B Vijay Mandal
New Delhi-110016

6th June, 20____

The President
India International Centre
New Delhi-110003

Sir

I take this opportunity to submit my application dated 24th March, 20____ for membership of the IIC. This is in compliance with your suggestion to me to apply for membership of IIC while releasing my book "Sunder Lekhan." I hope the application receives the favour and attention of the selection committee.

I shall be grateful if you will kindly recommend my application for membership.

With best regards

Yours faithfully

(Ashish Bajaj)

9. A letter of complaint to the Municipal Corporation

C-202 Malviya Nagar
New Delhi-110016

10th October, 20____

The Health Officer (South Zone)
The Municipal Corporation of Delhi
New Delhi-110016

Sub: Insanitary conditions in Malviya Nagar (C Block)

Sir

On behalf of the residents' association of Malviya Nagar, I would like to bring to your kind notice that our locality is suffering from insanitary conditions. The residents are afraid this may lead to an epidemic.

The sweepers do not attend to their duties and the garbage collection vans turn up only once a week. As a result, all the streets are full of garbage. Even the parks and open spaces are overflowing with garbage. The drains are also choked, which is causing stagnation of waste water. These have become the harbours of mosquitoes and insects. It is requested that the sanitary staff be intimated to attend to this locality on an emergency basis.

We hope that you will kindly take necessary action urgently and supervise the work personally. A copy of this letter is being endorsed to the MLA of the area for his kind information.

Thanking you

Yours faithfully

(Sonia Sharma)
for
Malviya Nagar Residents' Association

Copy to:
Sh. Dhan Raj, M.L.A.
Malviya Nagar
New Delhi

INFORMAL LETTERS

1. A letter to mother from hostel, describing how you have been doing there

Room No. 180
Boys' Hostel
Delhi Public School
Mathura Road
New Delhi-110003

15th September, 20____

My darling Mummy

Please don't worry Mom, I arrived comfortably at the hostel last night. I have already settled down in my room and had a good sleep. Everything was prearranged and taken care of. We were received by the hostel warden and taken to our rooms. Hot food and cosy beds were waiting for us. The affectionate attitude of the hostel staff largely mitigated my feeling of homesickness and strangeness of the new environment. However, I am prepared to step into a new world, where one has to live on his own; without the omnipresent care and love of parents, brothers or sisters.

I am sharing a room with two other boys, Shomit and Kapil. They seem to be studious and serious, although it is too early to judge. I will write about them in my next letter.

Tomorrow, we have a football match. Being in the hostel, one has the advantage of better participation in sports. But trust me, I will not do this at the cost of my studies. I always had the impression that hostel food is bland and tasteless. I am wondering if this popular impression is only a myth. If you believe me, the food here is not only tasty but also nutritious. We are given ample food, milk, fruits and salads. This morning, I had my favourite chole bhature for breakfast. Maybe, I am liking the hostel food only as a change, but certainly it is not as bad as we thought it would be.

I miss you the most. In spite of the comforts and the busy routine, I feel desolate without you, daddy and my dear sister Iti. How is daddy's backache? I hope he is better and going to his office. I pray to God to give health and happiness to my dear parents. Tell Iti that I am as lonely as she would be without me. Anyway, I will be coming home only after three months during the winter vacations.

I am also missing my friends in the neighbourhood, especially Ravi and Rajat. It is really painful to abandon everything and start building afresh, from scratch.

Let me stop before I start crying and make you cry. Cheer up and write soon.

Your love and soul

Ankur

2. A letter of well being to your mother

Anuj Kumar
Delhi Public School
Mathura Road
New Delhi-110003

June 7th, 20____

Dear Mom

How are you doing? Everything is fine with me.

I'm sorry that I haven't written for a while, but I've been really busy. As you know, I really like computers, and I'm spending long hours in front of the screen, both at work and at home.

In fact, I just bought a great programme. It's a neat collection of business letters that I can customise any way I want. For example, there's a letter to people who are late in paying their bills and another one that complains about a defective product.

I'm sure it'll save me a lot of time and energy—you know how hard it is for me to write a letter. Now I'll be able to think about business instead of worrying about what to say in a letter.

Too bad they don't have one for writing to you. Ha ha ha! They should also have one for thanking Lata Aunty for the cookies! Nah-formal letter could never replace the personal touch!

Gotta run now, Mom! All my love!

Yours lovingly

Anuj

3. A letter to sister giving home news

9-B Vijay Mandal
New Delhi-110016
18th August, 20____

My dearest Karuna

I was thrilled to get your beautiful *rakhi*, all the way from Muscat. Also, it was very sweet to read the letter written by your tender little hands. So nice to know that now you can write. Fondly remembering you, I tied your *rakhi*. You will get a nice *rakhi* gift whenever we meet. This is my promise. I know you need nothing but it will be my pleasure.

Iti is fine and remembers you. She was not too happy,

as you did not mention her in your letter. Mummy and daddy are also well and remember you very much. How are dear aunty and uncle. We all miss them. Mummy, daddy and Iti send their regards to them.

I am doing all right in my studies and sports. Now, I am the house captain. It is an exciting reponsibility.

How is your school? Do you have friends to play with? I am sure, you must be having many as everyone loves you.

Reply soon and tell me about Oman, your school and friends.

Yours lovingly

Ankur

4. A letter to your sister, describing your trip

C8/150 SDA
New Delhi-110016
2nd December, 20____

My dear Isha

I hope you are hale and hearty. you must be busy preparing for your examinations. I wish you best of luck for success with flying colours.

In this letter, I am going to share with you the story of an abandoned farmhouse, which I discovered in my latest adventure.

Last Sunday, my friends and I went trekking in the country side. It was a lovely day. After two hours of trekking, we were tired, hungry and thirsty. There we saw a farmhouse in ruins. We went to it hopping to find someone. The derelict building looked deserted. It was surrounded by wild grass, and the ground was lined up with boulders and stones. There was a rusty tractor under the shed. We knocked at the door. There was no reply.

We pushed our way into the farmhouse. The building was covered by spiderwebs and dust. Our curiosity and excitement of exploration made us forget our thirst and hunger. We proceeded towards the bedroom, which had a large single bed. The room was neatly painted in white. The windows were curtained. The kitchen was empty but there was a bottom of plum jam. The floor was carpeted. It was covered with dust. The almirah was empty.

Suddenly we realised that one of our friends Gaurav, was missing. We started looking for him. Then one of the doors creaked open. Something dark fumbled along. Rahul saw it first and watched it until all eyes were attracted towards it. The creature was fully covered with dust and looked as old as the farmhouse. Suddenly he started calling us by our names. We were shaking with fear. But soon we regained our senses and found that it was Gaurav. He had wandered into the fuel room and fallen on coal dust. He looked like a chimney sweep.

After this we all laughed heartily. We were amused and kept talking about various findings in the farmhouse. It was indeed a very interesting trip.

Tell me about your trip to Nepal. Did you have any adventure? It is very interesting to share the explorations of the long voyage of life. I will be coming back home after a month, during my summer vacations. I hope mummy and daddy are fine. Convey my regards to them.

Bye

With love

Akash

5. A letter of diwali greetings

44 Lajpat Nagar Part-1
New Delhi

17th October, 20____

Dear Prateesh

May this festival of lights bring a beam of happiness and a ray of hope in your life. Let the light sweep away the clouds of gloom and ignorance. Let the light always be with you, to shine like a star in the sky.

With compliments and best wishes for diwali.

Yours truly

(Sikhar Chand)

6. A letter replying to diwali greetings

29 Lodhi Road
New Delhi-110001

3rd November, 20____

Dear Sonal

It was a pleasant surprise to receive your greeting card

on the auspicious ocassion of diwali after a long time. It is nice to know that you still remember me.

I hope you are enjoying good health and studies. My sister, Iti, joins me in wishing you and your parents a bright and prosperous diwali.

With regards

Yours sincerely

(Aman)

7. A letter of new year greetings

2054 Mahatma Gandhi Road
New Delhi

30th December, 20___

Dear Prabha

May this new year bring joy and happiness to your life. Glow like the sun and enjoy good health and high spirits throughout the year.

Isha joins me in sending her warmest regards and greetings for the new year. Not only 1st January, but every day of the year may be a bright new day for you.

With love

Yours affectionately

(Rakhi Sehgal)

8. A letter replying to the new year greetings

18 Himalayan Apartment
Dehradun

2nd January, 20____

Dear Rohan

Many thanks for your kind greetings on the very onset of the new year. I am overwhelmed by your affection.

I take this opportunity to wish you a very happy new year.

With best wishes

Sincerely

(Sohan)

9. A letter of birthday greetings

202 Alakananda
Srinagar

11th August, 20____

Dear Shruti

Many happy returns of the day, may this day bring all the joys, success and fame to your life.

August 13th is a day for which I always wait. For it is your birthday. I wish I could have been with you on this day. Alas, I cannot come as I am too far away. Anyway, I am sending a watch separately by a registered parcel. I know how desperate you were for a watch last time. I hope you like this small token of my love.

With best wishes

Your Uncle

10. A letter of thanks for birthday present

18 Himalayan Apartment
Rajpur Road
Dehradun

18th March, 20____

My dear Uncle

I received your nice gift and greetings for my birthday. Your affectionate and inspiring words have always been special to me. Along with such a lovely gift, these have been even more precious. I received many presents but none was more beautiful than your watch. I needed it, and was very surprised to get one from you. I never imagined that my wish would be fulfilled so soon. Thank you for your affection and gift which I shall cherish forever.

My regards to dear aunty and love to Shalini and Priyanka.

Your loving niece

(Shruti)

11. A letter of thanks for invitation

Nilgiri Apartment
New Delhi

26th March, 20____

Dear Ashutosh

Thank you very much for inviting me for the picnic. I always love to go on picnics with you, as I know how interesting and innovative these are. I am really sorry as

I cannot make up for the picnic this time, because of my examination on the following day. Yes, exams are terrible and boring. Anyway go ahead and enjoy your picnic. I promise to join you next time. Do write to me about your picnic.

With love

Yours lovingly

(Vineet)

12. A letter of thanks for an invitation to an exhibition

24 Lajpat Nagar Part-II
New Delhi

August 5th, 20____

Dear Shobha

Thank you for your special invitation for your paintings on Rajasthan, displayed at Yamini Art Gallery, Hauz Khas.

It was indeed a privilege to visit the exhibition and view your superb paintings. We wish you all the success and many more such exhibitions.

With regards

Sincerely

(Rakhi)

13. A letter of greetings on marriage

24 Tagore Park
New Delhi-110006

6th March, 20____

Dear Mr and Mrs Manglik

We are happy to receive the invitation for the auspicious ocassion of the marriage of your dear daughter, Vartika with Sudhir. We congratulate you on performing the divine ceremony and hope that the marriage is solemnised with grace and happiness. We will come on the day of marriage to wish the newly weds.

We pray to God to bless the newly weds.

Regards

Sincerely

(Mrs V. K. Gaur)

14. A letter of compliments on marriage

12 D Vijay Enclave
New Delhi

9th December, 20____

My dear Rishabh

We are overwhelmed by your gesture of remembering and inviting us to share the pleasant and auspicious occasion of the marriage of you dear sister Bhavana.

Though we are unable to join the ceremony, due to certain preoccupation, we wish the newly weds a very happy life. We hope that Bhavana is happy. We hope that Bhavana will find an equally affectionate environment in her new home.

With best wishes and regards

Yours sincerely

(Ajay Sharma)

15. A letter of congratulations

15 Rajendra Nagar
New Delhi

12th November, 20____

Dear Saurabh

Yesterday was a day of big surprises. I could never imagine that the newspaper would print your photograph with the president of India. So, my friend, you are a celebrity and it calls for a celebration. Out of millions, you are among the distinguished sixteen children, who have been chosen for the Bravery Medal by the highest authority of the land, i.e. the president of India. You earned it. I knew you would make it one day, when you saved a little girl from the wheels of a reversing bus and got your wrist bone fractured. You have made me, your friends, teachers and our school proud. I express my happiness at this moment. My sister and other friends add to 'three cheers'. They are all waiting to congratulate you personally, when the school reopens. We are eagerly waiting to see you riding an elephant at the Republic Day Parade. Keep it up.

With best wishes

Yours affectionately

Manish

16. A letter of congratulations on getting admission in the IIT

44 New Rajendra Nagar
New Delhi

1st July, 20____

Dear Amarish

You can hardly imagine my delight when Anuj told me that you have got through the IIT examination and secured 20th position in All India ranking. It must surely give you a feeling of victory to have reached this dizzying height. Now the golden gates of opportunities lie open before you.

You fully deserve this success. You have always been a fine student and worked hard to achieve what you desired. Your sincere efforts have rewarded you.

Your aunty and Rasika join the chorus in congratulating you on your achievement. We are proud of you. Keep it up.

Yours affectionately

(Vivek)

17. A letter of congratulations on birth of a baby girl

24 K.G. Marg
New Delhi-110001

24th July, 20____

Dear Madhuri

The great news has just filtered through Manjusha that you have given birth to a healthy baby girl. I am really excited. Accept our heariest congratulations on your attaining motherhood.

A girl of such a intelligent mother will no doubt carve a brilliant pathway in life. Give our warmest love to the little one, and take care of your health. Do let me know what name you have decided to give to the baby.

Yours affectionately

(Karuna)

18. A letter of condolence to a friend in grief

55-F Kailash Park
New Delhi

4th August, 20_____

My dear Abhinav

I am writing this letter to you with a heavy heart. And it is natural when one has to share the grief of a dear friend. I am shocked to have just heard that your mother expired last week. No tragedy can be greater. It became even more distressing and deep when I remember your mother. She was the personification of ultimate nobility, affection and devotion. There are no words to console you in this agony. There is nothing in the world which can fill the void of a mother. A son feels as if a part of him has died. One feels a gap in the deep bondage of the souls of a son and a mother.

I pray to God to give peace to the departed soul and strength to all of you to bear the harsh blow. I hope that the wheel of life continues to rotate and cycle of grief will pass with peace and silence.

May God be with you.

Your friend in grief

(Aryan)

19. A letter to a friend, describing an interesting event

813 Vijay Enclave
New Delhi-110050

1st September, 20____

Dear Ankush

How are you? Everything is fine here. Lots of love to your sister Manisha and deep respects to Uncle and Aunty.

Have you ever been to a marriage? Certainly yes, you would have been to many marriages. But you would not have been to one as grand as the one I went to on Sunday. It was a very interesting event and I am eager to tell you.

It was my father's friend's daughter's marriage. Everything seemed so nice, beautiful and larger than life. There was a huge tent, which was a replica of some royal palace, with marvellous decoration. It was a theme marriage and the theme was era 1960s. Everyone had to come dressed up according to fashion of 1960s. Even I wore a dress of 1960s fashion. There was a huge gathering, approximately 2000 people were there.

Musicians and dancers from different parts of the world presented spectacular performance. There were more than 200 different kinds of cuisines from Thai, Italian, Chinese, Mughlai, continental to South Indian and North Indian. You won't believe there were more than 2000 varieties of fruits and desserts from across the globe.

The pretty bride came in a royal *palkhi* (palanquin), she looked like an angel. The bridegroom came in an helicopter, like a film hero and landed right in the middle of tent where a small temporary helipad was made. Afterwards the marriage took place with all rituals and tradition.

This was the first time that I witnessed such a big Indian wedding. Have you ever witnessed such a spectacular marriage? Do tell me about it.

Waiting for your reply.

Yours sincerely

Abhay

20. A letter to your friend, inviting him to spend the vacations with you

3-B Jawahar Nagar
Delhi-110007

26th April, 20____

Dear Prateek

I congratulate you on your passing the examinations with flying colours. I think you deserve a nice treat after such hard work. I have a proposal. Why don't you come to Delhi and spend some time with us? After that we will go to Manali for trekking. I know that you love nature and enjoy trekking. This would be a wonderful relaxation.

I have already chalked out a programme for your stay in Delhi and subsequent visit to Manali. I have contacted the youth hostel, which is organising a trip for amateur trekkers. The trip starts from Delhi on 10th May and is for ten days. So please confirm your participation at the earliest.

Awaiting an early reply.

Yours lovingly

(Ravi Kumar)

21. A letter to a friend, inviting him on dussehra festival

150 Safdarjung Development Area
New Delhi-110016

15th October, 20____

Dearest Prateek

Although I haven't received any reply to my last letter, I couldn't wait as I am so excited. I thought let me write myself and share my joy. Yes, I am thrilled with a different kind of celebration of dussehra, which we are organising ourselves. Dussehra is perhaps the most popular festival among us. It is fascinating and action-packed. Every year, we used to go to see *ramlila* at the Ramlila Grounds. This year my friends and I thought why not celebrate it ourselves. We have planned the celebration which will be held in our colony. The entire planning and arrangements are being made by our group of ten friends, without the help of elders. We will have various activities and lots of fun, which include a fete with games, eatables etc. We will also have a music and cultural programme. At the end we will burn the effigies of Ravana, Meghnada and Kumbhkarana. We will be making effigies ourselves and will be filling them with lots of crackers. For convenience, we have divided the work amongst ourselves.

It is very exciting to get the support and encouragement from everyone. Within one day, we collected rupees ten thousand for expenses.

So you see, this is going to be a grand and gala affair. You should come to this great occasion and enjoy the festival with us. I am sending an invitation for you and your family.

Looking forward to see you.

Yours lovingly

Akash

22. A letter to your friend, inviting him to celebrate new year with you

180 Asian Games Village
New Delhi-110049

12th December, 20____

My dear Sumit

Bang-Bang! Yes, this is the time to rejoice. It is time to say goodbye to 20____ and welcome the New Year 20____. We are planning to enter 20____ with a big bang.

We have planned to celebrate the new year by having a party in our garden. Yes, it will be midnight and cold. For this we will have a big bonfire. Around this, we will be playing and dancing, singing, drinking and eating.

My daddy brought some records and CDs of Michael Jackson and Freddie Mercury from England. They are the latest and just marvellous. I am sure that you, I and everyone would start dancing to this thrilling music. Exactly when the clock strikes 12.00, we will burst crackers. Naturally, everyone would wish each other a happy new year. This is how we are planning to celebrate our new year.

I hope you can come and join us. Your presence will, of course, double the fun.

Regards to your parents. I hope you bring your sister along with you. Waiting for a 'yes' from you.

With love

Ankit

23. A letter to a friend, inviting him on your birthday

174 Tagore Park
Delhi

9th August, 20____

Dear Pranav

I hope this letter finds you in good health and high spirits.

Again we will have the Independence Day. This is a very important day for all Indians. But wait, just two days before that we have another red letter day. This is my birthday and I hope you remember this day rather well. We are going to celebrate it in a unique and amazing manner. I am not going to tell you anything right now about the surprises we are going to have, so that you keep turning in your bed and anxiously look forward to be with us on the 13th. Let me tell you, the great event will start in the morning at 9 and not in the evening. So be ready.

You may like to note it down in your diary right now. You never know when the mobile network goes off and if so, you may not get a telephonic reminder.

So get ready to celebrate the birthday of a great man (modesty is not my trait) who happens to be your friend.

Looking forward to see you.

Yours lovingly

Manav

24. A letter to a friend, describing about your vacation

B-40 Kirti Nagar
New Delhi

10th July, 20____

Dear Sayantan

I hope you still remember me. We met in Bangalore. We came so close in just four days. Perhaps because we had something in common and yet were so different. Those moments in Bangalore are memories which, I hope, will remain for life.

For the past few days I was busy with my vacation homework. Thank God it is over just in time. Our school reopened on the 3rd of July. It again is the same routine of tests, homework and all that.

How is your violin practice going on? I have a lot of interest in music. Inspired by you, I also want to join the Trinity College of Music. I would be grateful if you could give me some information on how and where to apply, the fees, what the course is all about and the procedure of learning etc.

Nowadays, I am reading an interesting book called 'The Gaia Atlas of Future Worlds' by Norman Myers. It is about global changes in the environment, structures, politics, ideas, beliefs, science and technology. It represents holistic approaches to the gathering human and ecological crisis. I would recommend that you read it too, if you get the chance.

Our social work organisation is yet to start. We are planning to meet sometime next week and decide our line of action.

I received lovely letters from Sharmila and Kuntal Das. Kriti, Pooja and Muneet talked to me on the phone. They are all fine and remember each other.

Do write back whenever you get time. Also please write about the Trinity College of Music.

Yours ever

Rahul

25. A letter to a friend, asking about his trip

126 Preet Vihar
Delhi

2nd July, 20____

Dear Sayantan

How was your trip to France? After Bangalore, France must have been so different. How did your concert go? I am sure you must have got a big applause for your performance. I am sure that French men and women are encouraging and loving. Perhaps, the only difficulty would have been the language barrier. As far as music is concerned it knows no language, it cuts across all language barriers and touches the heart.

How is your piano practice going on? I am sending notes of 'A Country Boy Can Survive' by Hank Williams. I hope these are useful to you.

Please write all about your trip to France. I would be eagerly looking forward to your letter.

Best of luck and love

Rahul

26. A letter to a friend, describing your new car

B-240 Shastri Nagar
New Delhi

7th February, 20____

Dearest Kunal

Hope you are in the best of your spirits and health. It's been long that you dropped me a word or two.

I am super excited these days as my dad has bought a new car last week. It is a two seater electric car. You must be wondering why do we need a two seater car? My dad bought it since it would serve as an additional mode of transportation when only one or two members of our family have to travel. The new car is fuel saving as it runs on electrically charged batteries. It saves us the trouble of getting stuck on a narrow road. Our other car is a five seater which normally gets stuck in a traffic jam or on a narrow road. The new car runs as fast and as efficiently as any normal diesel or petrol car. Electric car do not pollute the environment since no fuel burns and no smoke is emitted.

Hope you visit my place soon to experience the pleasure of travelling in an electric car.

Do reply, with a plan to visit my place, soon.

Convey my regards to grandma, uncle, aunt and tight hug to little Ashu.

Your loving friend

Karan Singh

27. A letter to a friend, congratulating him for a new car

Pocket 5, F-26
Rohini
New Delhi

10th February, 20____

Dear Karan

Hello! I hope you are enjoying new car rides every day. Please accept my heartiest congratulations for your new car. I am as excited and thrilled as you are to hear about your electric car. I hope to see it soon. Sorry for not being able to write for a long time, I had my mid term examinations which kept me busy for a long time. I have performed rather well in my exams and hope to get a good result.

What colour is your new car? Probably you forgot to mention it due to your excitement. I would plan a visit very soon and then I would tell you my experience about driving in your electric car. I have thought of a name for your electric car, 'Electrica'. How does it sound to you?

Do reply to me about your schedule for next week so that I can plan my visit to your place accordingly.

Convey my congratulations to uncle and aunt, too.

Awaiting your early reply and hope to catch you soon.

Your dearest friend

Kunal

APPLICATIONS

1. An application for leave

Sector 5
Rohini
New Delhi

25th October, 20____

The Principal
Delhi Public School
Mathura Road
New Delhi-110003

Sub: Application for leave

Sir

You would be proud to know that the undersigned, a student of class X-G of your school, has won second prize in the Asian Children's Art Competition organised by the government of Japan. The prize distribution ceremony will be held in Tokyo on 8th December, 20____. My air ticket for Japan has been arranged by the Japan Embassy in New Delhi. You are kindly requested to grant me leave for five days, i.e. from 5th December to 10th December, 20____, so that I can attend the prize distribution function. I am sure that my attendance in the ceremony shall bring laurels to the school and our country.

Thanking you

Yours obediently

(Ankur Jain)
Class X-G

2. An application for remission of fine

C-117
Lakeview Apartment
New Delhi

23rd December, 20____

The Principal
Central School
Arya Samaj Road
New Delhi-110003

Sub: Remission of fine

Respected Sir

I humbly want to state that a fine of Rs. 200/- has been imposed on me for reaching the school late yesterday. I agree that this is against discipline, but the circumstances under which I got late were beyond my control.

I started on my bicycle from my house at the usual time. Near the railway crossing, I saw an old woman bleeding profusely. It seemed that some vehicle had hit her and run. I took the woman to Sir Ganga Ram Hospital and had her admitted in the casualty ward. I thought the victim deserved priority over the routine, as it was a question of her life and death. It was only after I was assured by the hospital staff the she was out of danger, and her relatives arrived, that I could leave the hospital. That is why I was late to school by three hours. However, when I reached the school the gatekeeper did not allow me to enter unless the permission was obtained from the head boy. The head boy did not listen to me and imposed a fine of Rs. 200/-.

Most humbly, I request you to kindly order the withdrawal of the fine, in view of the facts given above. I assure you of my strict adherence to the school discipline always.

Thanking you

Yours obediently

(Suresh Manchanda)
Class X-B

3. An application for scholarship

398 Sunder Vihar
New Delhi

4th January, 20____

The Principal
Model School
Daya Basti

Sub: Requesting for scholarship

Sir

With due respect, I submit that I am a student of class VIII-C of your school. I belong to a poor family. My father, who was head clerk in the railways, retired last month. This has brought calamity to our family. With his meagre pension of Rs. 3,000/- p.m., he has to feed the entire family besides housing, clothing and education. It is becoming very difficult for me to continue my education, which is beyond our affordability. However, I am very keen to continue my studies in your school.

As you know, I am not only a good student, but the captain of the junior football team as well. I have brought laurels to the school in inter-school debate competitions. My keen ambition is to pursue higher studies for serving the nation as a doctor.

I would be grateful, if you kindly waive the fees and grant me a merit-cum-means scholarship. I am sure you would find me most deserving of this. Your kindness would permit me to continue my studies, and to fulfil my dream of becoming a doctor. I will always cherish your kindness. I am confident that you will kindly grant me a scholarship.

Thanking you

Yours obediently

Gautam Pal
Class VIII-C

4. Draft an application for the post of senior programmer on behalf of Mr Shivam Kishore, give all necessary details.

Shivam Kishore
Ridgeview Apartments
Mathura Road
New Delhi-110003

7th June, 20____

Mr. Anil Kumar
The Vice President
ITC Ltd.
New Delhi

Sub: Application for the post of senior programmer

Sir

I am interested in working as a senior programmer for your organisation. I am an expert programmer with over ten years of experience. I enclose my resume as a first step in exploring the possibility of employment with your company.

My most recent experience was designing an automated billing system for a trade magazine publisher. I was responsible for the overall product design, including the user interface. In addition, I developed the first draft of the operator's guide.

As a senior programmer with your organisation, I will bring a focus on quality and user friendly system. Furthermore, I work well with others, and am experienced in project management.

I will appreciate your keeping this enquiry confidential. I shall be available for the interview as and when called.

Hoping for a favourable reply.

Yours faithfully

(Shivam Kishore)

5. An application for change of optional subject

Q 52 Phase I
Kings' Lane
Kathmandu

4th April, 20____

The Principal
St. Joseph Public School
Lakeview Road
Kathmandu

Sub: Requesting for change of an optional subject

Sir

Humble request is that I Bhuvan Chowdhry of class XI-C of your institution wants to change my optional subject. Sir I opted for physical education, as this suited me the best out of available options but now that there is a new optional subject available, i.e. Media Studies, I was like to opt for it. Sir, I would like to explore the new avenues available in the field of media hence, I want to study the subject, media studies. Sir, kindly allow me to do the same.

I will be highly thankful to you.

Thanking you

Yours obediently

(Bhauvan Chowdhry)
Class XI-C

6. An application for issuing a character certificate

Pocket 5, Block 1
Bank Street
Lahore
Ph: ________

25th June, 20____

The Principal
Islamic Public School
Bank Street
Lahore

Sub: Requesting for a character certificate

Sir

Kind request is that I have passed out from class XII from your school, with this year's batch. Sir, now I need to apply to various colleges for pursuing my higher studies and I would need a character certificate from the school to get admission to any reputed college or course. Sir, I bear a good moral character and was a good student throughout my schooling. The facts can be verified from the school records and my former teachers. Sir, kindly issue me a character certificate at the earliest and oblige.

Thanking you

Yours obediently

(Ahmed Khan)
Batch 20____ to 20____

7. An application requesting a change of section

H.no. 567
Phasc III
Royal Estate
Colombo

10th March, 20____

The Principal
St. August Convent School
Institutional Area
Colombo

Sub: Requesting for change of section

Madam

I have the honour to request you that I Jatin David is student of class IX-B of your institution. Madam, kind request is that I want to change my class section from 'B' to 'C'. My twin sister, Tina David studies in our school in class IX-C. Since we are siblings and we are in same class and live in the same house, we share the same set of reference books and other such resources. My father cannot afford two sets of reference books for us. Please kindly allow me to change my section from 'B' to 'C', in the light of above facts, so that me and my sister can study well together.

Please oblige by doing the needful.

Thanking you

Yours obediently

(Jatin David)
Class IX-B
Roll No. 52

8. An application for full fee concession

Flat no. 250
Sector 5
Paradise Enclave
Dhaka

15th July, 20____

The Principal
Government Senior Secondary School
Seaside Colony
Dhaka

Sub: Requesting for full fee concession

Sir

I Sanya Malik of class X-C of your school humbly request you for a full fee concession of the school tuition fee. Sir, I belong to a lower middle class family with six members and my father being the sole breadwinner with a meagre salary of Rs 5000 per month. It gets very difficult for him to even provide basic needs to all the family members. Now that the inflation rate is touching sky he has no other option left but to stop my schooling. I have been always been a good student and the same can be verified from my class teacher and the school records. Sir, education is must for all and I want to be well educated to serve my nation in the capacity of an astronaut. Hope my financial constrain does not obstruct my noble goal of education and knowledge.

Thanking you

Yours obediently

(Sanya Malik)
Class X-C
Roll No. 21

9. An application for issuing an experience certificate

Flat no. 52
LIG Flats
Safdarjung Enclave
New Delhi-110029
Ph: ________

20th July, 20____

Senior Officer (HR)
TCL Pvt. Ltd.
B-11059 Sector 12
Noida
Uttar Pradesh-201301

Sub: Requesting for an experience certificate

Madam

Humble request is that I Nikhil Anand served your organisation in the capability of manager (finance). I have recently resigned from the same post and have served required one month's notice. Please kindly issue me a service experience certificate, mentioning my date of joining, date of reliving, the post, salary and moral conduct therein, at the earliest.

Please do the needful and oblige.

Thanking you

Yours faithfully

(Nikhil Anand)

10. An application for issuing a duplicate marksheet

Y-248 Block B
Queens' Lane
Dhaka
Ph: ________

25th May, 20____

The Director
Central Board of Examinations
Institutional Area
Dhaka

Sub: Requesting for issuing a duplicate marksheet

Sir/Madam

Humble request is I, Dhirsti Maidan have lost my Senior Secondary Examination (original) marksheet. I lost the marksheet when I was returning from an office after applying for a vacancy there. A thief snatched away my purse, when I was waiting for the bus at the bus stop.

The purse carried my some important documents along with the marksheet. I have already lodged a FIR for the same. Please issue me a duplicate marksheet at the earliest. The details of my student records can be taken down from the photocopy of the marksheet attached herewith. I have also enclosed a demand draft dated 25th July, 20____, amount ______________, in your favour, in lieu of the fee for issuing the duplicate marksheet.

Please do the needful and oblige.

Thanking you

Yours faithfully

(Dhirsti Maidan)

Encl: 1. Photocopy of marksheet
2. DD (in original)

11. An application to school requesting to change school bus route

250 Block B
Asian Village
New Delhi

3rd November, 20____

The Transport Officer
Delhi Public School
Mathura Road
New Delhi-110003

Sub: Requesting to change school bus route

Sir

The school bus (route no. 1-34A) has stopped coming to Asian Games Village suddenly. Recently, the traffic in Asian Games Village has been made one way, which entails a little longer route. While other school buses have followed the new traffic pattern, our bus (1- 34A) has preferred to pick up and drop the students outside the Asian Games Village, i.e. on Khel Gaon Marg, causing undue delay and walk of 700 m to 1 km. We shall be obliged if you kindly instruct the bus to continue with the picking up/dropping of students inside the Asian Games Village premises as before.

We shall be grateful for your kindness.

Thanking you

Yours faithfully

(Anand Raj)
Class X-B

Copy to: The Principal, Delhi Public School, Mathura Road

PART – V

NOTICE AND ADVERTISEMENT WRITING

NOTICE WRITING

The notice is meant to convey official information to a target group. It must convey all the necessary information in less words and simple language.

Guidelines

NOTICE WRITING FORMAT:

Following is the format of notice writing. Always enclose the notice in a box.

NOTICE
Name of the organisation
Date
TITLE OF NOTICE (in All Caps)
Body of the Notice (All Details)
Signature (of the person writing notice)
Name (of the person writing notice)
Designation (of the person writing notice)
Department and name of the organisation

Keypoints to remember:

- Always make a rough draft before writing the final notice.
- Take only important points from the question.

- Give only necessary details like date, venue and time.
- Stick to the given word limit.
- Do not add additional information.
- Language should be simple and notice should be short.
- Only formal but easy words should be used.
- Always enclose your notice in a box.
- Always give a title to your notice, it ensures targeted readability of the notice.
- Title should be crisp, short, eyecatching and appropriate.

EXAMPLES OF NOTICES

1. Your school is organising a singing competition in the school. Write a notice inviting entries for the same on behalf of the president of cultural society of your school. Incorporate all the necessary details.

NOTICE

Bhatnagar International School, Pitampura

10th November, 20____

SINGING COMPETITION

It is to hereby inform all the students of classes VI to XII that entries are invited for singing competition to be held on 28th November, 20____ in the school auditorium. Only Hindi/regional language patriotic songs both filmy and non-filmy are allowed. Interested students of classes VI to XII can give their names to the undersigned latest by 20th November, 20____. For further enquiries contact the undersigned.

(Signature)
Amit Tanwar
President, Cultural Society
Bhatnagar International School

2. Your school principal has decided to postpone the mid-term examinations. Write a notice about the same on behalf of your school principal. Give all the necessary details.

NOTICE

Senior Secondary Government School, Rohini

10th July, 20_____

MID-TERM EXAMS POSTPONED

All the students of classes V to XII are hereby informed that the 'Mid-term Examinations' which were to be held from 15th July, 20____ to 30th July, 20____ are postponed to undecided dates in month of August due to some unavoidable reasons. The fresh datesheet would be soon announced and students can contact their class teachers for further details. The prescribed course for the examination would remain same.

(Signature)
Anil Kumar
Principal
Senior Secondary Government School, Rohini

3. You lost your gold chain in school. Prepare a notice giving description of the chain and probable time of disappearance.

NOTICE

D.A.V. Public School, Vasant Vihar

25th July, 20____

LOST GOLD CHAIN

It is to hereby inform all the students and staff of the school that the undersigned has lost a gold chain, weighing about ten grams and about 45 cm long. It is a thin chain with a pendant with a photograph of Lord Shiva. It might have been lost on 20th July, 20____ during the cricket match between Ganga and Yamuna House teams. The finder would be suitably rewarded. Please contact the undersigned in case of any such finding.

(Signature)
Amita Agarwal
Class X-A
D.A.V. Public School

4. You found a wrist watch. Write a notice for the 'Lost and Found' noticeboard of your school.

NOTICE

Kendriya Vidyalaya, R.K. Puram

20th October, 20____

FOUND A WRIST WATCH

It is to hereby inform all the students and staff of the school that a wrist watch was found by the undersigned on 18th October, 20____ in the corridor of second floor near class XI-B. The owner may identify and collect the same from the undesigned at the earliest.

(Signature)
Prateesh Kumar
IX -A
Kendriya Vidyalaya, R.K. Puram

5. Write a notice on behalf of the president, residents welfare association, Paschim Vihar, informing the residents of your colony about power cuts in your colony. Give all the necessary details.

NOTICE

Residents Welfare Association, Paschim Vihar

20th December, 20____

SCHEDULED POWER CUTS

All the residents of Paschim Vihar are hereby informed that BSES has decided to have power cuts all over Delhi to save electricity for extra consumption in Commonwealth Games, 20____. We all should co-operate with the authorities. BSES has given us time schedule of 2 hours for power cuts i.e. 6 pm to 8 pm daily untill further notice. Please try to curtail your work accordingly. Inconvenience caused is regretted.

(Signature)
Anita Shaw
President
Residents Welfare Association, Paschim Vihar

ADVERTISEMENT WRITING

1. Your pet dog has disappeared from your house. Write a short description fit for the 'Lost and Found' column of the newspaper.

Lost and Found

Missing since 6th September, 20____ a Pomeranian, pure white female dog, one year old. Its height is about 14 inches. It has some black hair on the tail. Wearing a leather strap ASD no. K.F. 417. Finder will be suitably rewarded. Kindly contact Rahul Khanna, 15 D Panchsheel Enclave, New Delhi Ph.____

2. Write a classified advertisement for the 'Lost and Found' column of the newspaper, stating the loss of your briefcase containing important documents. Give details of the briefcase and its contents.

Lost And Found

Lost a red office briefcase while travelling by bus from Meerut to New Delhi on 26th March, 20____, between 7 am to 9 am. It contains my passport, an appointment letter for a job in the USA and other important documents. Finder may kindly contact Rohan Sharma, 418 Kavi Nagar, Meerut, Ph._______. Finder will be suitably rewarded and all his travel expenses will be paid on the spot in cash.

3. Write an advertisement for the 'Accommodation Wanted' column of a newspaper for hiring a bungalow for a Japanese family.

Accommodation Wanted

A Japanese multinational requires an independent bungalow with four bedrooms, drawing room, lobby and study, for its managing director, preferably in Jor Bagh,

Golf Links or Vasant Vihar, on company lease for three years. Contact phone: ________, Fax: _________

4. You want to let out a flat which is fully furnished, on rent. Write an advertisement to be published in a newspaper giving the essential details of the furnished accommodation, its location and expected rent.

To-Let

Available, accomodation at Hauz Khas. SFS, Duplex flat, fully furnished, with fridge, three air conditioners, colour television, telephone, furniture, carpets, washing machine and other furnishings; three bedrooms with terrace. Approximate area 1800 sq. feet. Expected rent around Rs. 20,000/-. Please contact H-120 SFS, Hauz Khas, Phone:________

5. A lady receptionist is required for a five star hotel. Write an advertisement for the 'Situation Vacant' column of a newspaper.

Situation Vacant

Required for a super deluxe five star hotel in New Delhi, a young lady receptionist. Well educated with pleasing personality, should be fluent in English and Hindi, with knowledge of a foreign language. Handsome salary with excellent perks. Apply in confidence with complete biodata to Box 243654-R, Hindustan Times, New Delhi-110001

6. Building is required on rent to start a garment export business. Write a suitable advertisement to be published in a local newspaper in the 'Wanted on Rent' column.

Wanted On Rent

Wanted on rent suitable and spacious building, approximately 3000 square feet area in New Delhi, for a garment export business. Rent negotiable. Location preferred—Kirti Nagar, Naraina, and Najafgarh Road. Interested parties may please contact on phone: ________

7. You want to let out a house on rent. Prepare an advertisement for publication in a newspaper, giving the location of the house, nature of accommodation and rent expected.

To–Let

Available, a newly constructed house in Defence Colony, 1st floor; drawing, dining, three bedrooms with attached toilets, kitchen, study and balcony. Approx. area 2200 sq. feet., expected rent Rs. 15,000/- per month. Contact phone: _________

8. Your brother, aged 8, has been missing since Wednesday 20th April, 20____. Write a suitable advertisement for the 'Lost Person' column of a newspaper.

Missing

Missing since 20th April, 20____, a boy named Ashish Garg, 8 years old, 4 feet 3 inches height, fair, chubby cheeks, healthy with curly hair, and a mole on the lips. He is wearing black shorts and red black striped T-shirt. Finder will be suitably rewarded. Contact Sanjay Garg, 1745 Vasant Kunj, phone: ________ or contact the nearest police station.

9. Your car was stolen from a parking lot in Connaught Place. Write a notice for 'Lost and Found' column of a newspaper.

Lost

Maruti Esteem AC, red colour, bearing registration number DCD A G 4516, with tape recorder, electronic clock and decorative steering. It was stolen on Tuesday, 17th May, 20____ from the parking lot of Inner Circle of Block C, Connaught Place. Finder will be suitably rewarded. Contact: Chetan Kumar, 47 Panchsheel Park, phone: ________, or SHO, Police Station, Parliament Street, New Delhi

10. Write an advertisement for the 'Situation Vacant' column of a newspaper for the post of lady private secretary to managing director of an advertisement agency.

Situation Vacant

A reputed advertisement agency requires a dynamic young lady private secretary to the managing director. She should be fluent in English and have knowledge of computer operations. Apply with complete biodata within one week to: M.S. Advertisement Agency, 54 Surya Building, K.G. Marg, New Delhi-110001, phone:________

11. You need a computer operator for your office. Write an advertisement for the 'Situation Vacant' column of a local newspaper.

Situation Vacant

Wanted an efficient and experienced computer operator for our New Delhi office. The candidate should be graduate and well versed in MS Office, with excellent command over English. Attractive salary, negotiable according to experience. Apply within 15 days to: Post Box no. 341675, The Times Of India, New Delhi-110002

12. You need a tutor for maths and science. Write an advertisement for a local daily.

Wanted Tutor

Wanted tutor to coach a class X student in maths and science. Handsome remuneration. Please contact within a week: Arjun Singh, 2 Pragati Vihar Hostel, New Delhi-110003

13. Write a matrimonial advertisement for a suitable match for your daughter, to be published in a local daily.

For Grooms

Alliance required for Punjabi Girl, 24 Years, 5' 4", fair, slim, M.Sc., lecturer in a reputed college, hails from rich respectable family. Boy should be well educated and well settled, preferably a doctor, architect or engineer. Box 75525-CA, Hindustan Times, New Delhi-110001

14. Write a matrimonial advertisement for your son, working in a multinational company.

For Brides

Wanted pretty, slim, well educated Khatri girl for an engineer, 5'10", handsome boy, working with a multinational company. Monthly income in five figures. Please apply to Post Box: 15184-CA, Hindustan Times, New Delhi-110001

NOTES

NOTES

NOTES